Worksheets
For use with

EXPLORING DRAFTING

FUNDAMENTALS OF DRAFTING TECHNOLOGY

BY

JOHN R. WALKER   BERNARD D. MATHIS

Publisher

The Goodheart-Willcox Company, Inc.

Tinley Park, Illinois

www.g-w.com

Introduction

The worksheets in this student supplement enrich and reinforce the material presented in *Exploring Drafting*. They are intended to help you develop problem-solving ability. Problems selected from the text are presented in order of increasing difficulty. Using these worksheets helps to eliminate repetitive drawing, and enables you to get directly into problem-solving situations.

Drawing numbers shown to the right of the title blocks key the drawing to chapters in *Exploring Drafting*. For example, information that will aid in solving Problem 6-1 can be found in Chapter 6. Blank worksheets in the back may be used for special assignments.

John R. Walker

Bernard D. Mathis

Sketch a problem assigned by your instructor.

Sketching Problem

Name

Date

Sketch a problem assigned by your instructor.

Sketching Problem

Name

Date

Sketch a problem assigned by your instructor.

Sketching Problem

Name

Date

Draw an ellipse using the concentric circle method.

Major axis = $5\frac{1}{2}''$
Minor axis = $4''$

Ellipse Construction	Date

Name

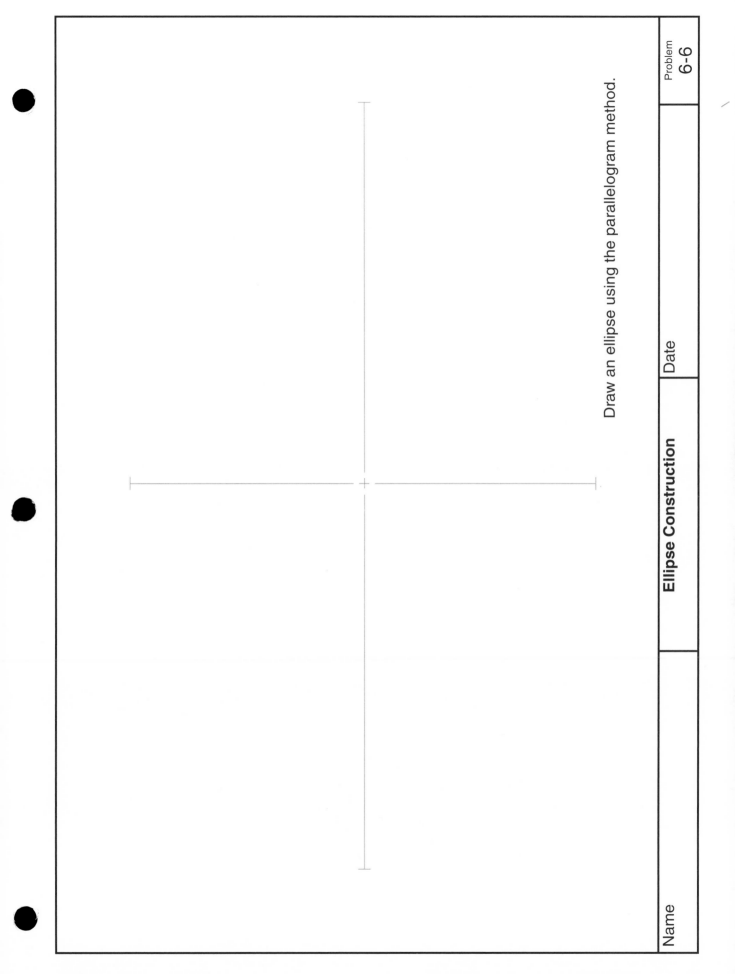

Draw an ellipse using the parallelogram method.

Name		Date
Ellipse Construction		Problem 6-6

Draw an ellipse using the four-center approximate method.

Date

Ellipse Construction

Name

Draw a United States aircraft insignia with a 4" diameter star.

Design Problem

Problem
6-8

Name

Date

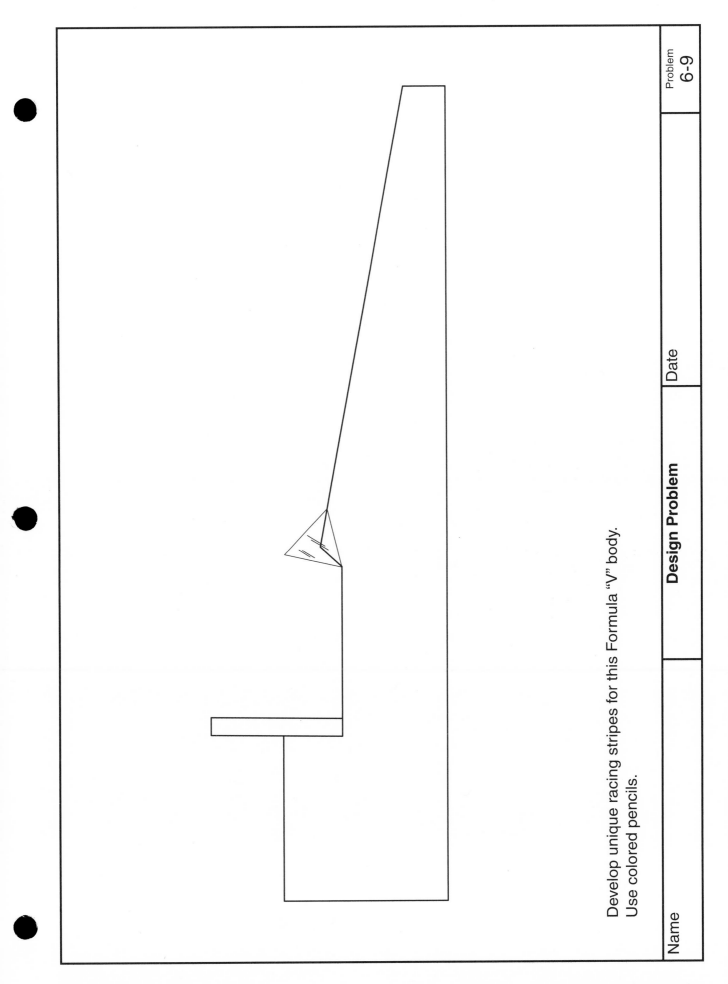

Develop unique racing stripes for this Formula "V" body. Use colored pencils.

Name

Date

Design Problem

Problem 6-9

A GOOD DRAFTER LETTERS
NEATLY AND RAPIDLY.

YOUR NAME
YOUR SCHOOL

Date

Lettering Practice

Name

THE QUICK RED FOX JUMPED

OVER THE LAZY BROWN DOG.

1 2 3 4 5 6 7 8 9 0 $\frac{1}{2}$ $\frac{1}{16}$ $\frac{3}{8}$ $\frac{5}{32}$

Copyright by Goodheart-Willcox Co., Inc.

Name

Date

Lettering Practice

MAKE THE MOST OF YOURSELF

FOR THAT IS ALL THERE IS OF

YOU.

"THE BEST THING ABOUT THE

FUTURE IS THAT IT COMES ONE

DAY AT A TIME."

Copyright by Goodheart-Willcox Co., Inc.

Date

Lettering Practice

Name

PACK EACH BOX WITH SEVEN

DOZEN GIANT JUGS.

1 2 3 4 5 6 7 8 9 0 1 3 5 7
2 4 8 9

Date

Name

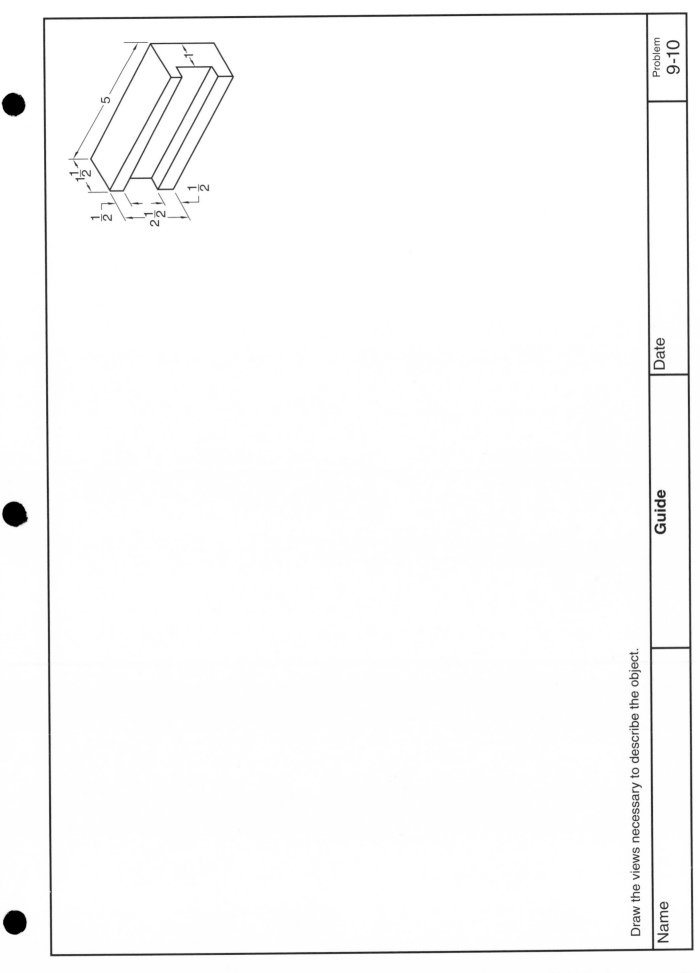

Date

Guide

Draw the views necessary to describe the object.

Name

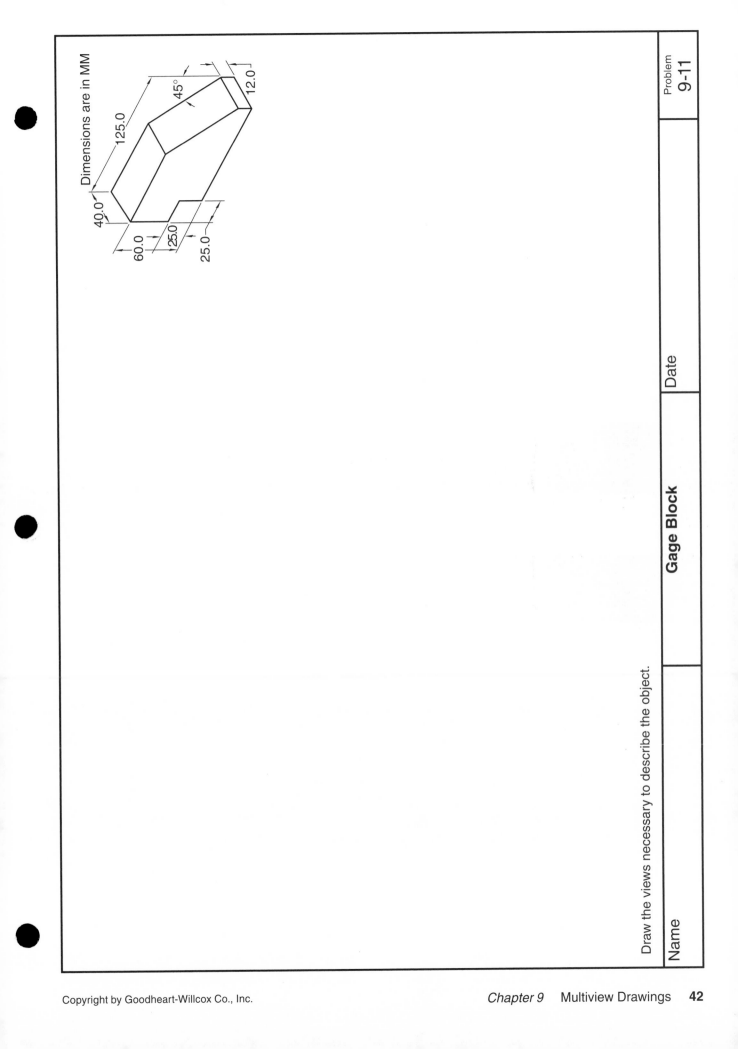

Dimensions are in MM

125.0

45°

12.0

40.0

60.0

25.0

25.0

Draw the views necessary to describe the object.

Gage Block

Name

Date

R1¼
4
2
1½
2½

Draw the views necessary to describe the object.

Name

Guide Block

Date

45°

$1\frac{1}{2}$

4

$\frac{1}{2}$(TYP.)

$\frac{3}{4}$

$\frac{3}{4}$

$2\frac{1}{2}$

Draw the views necessary to describe the object.

Name

Angled Guide

Date

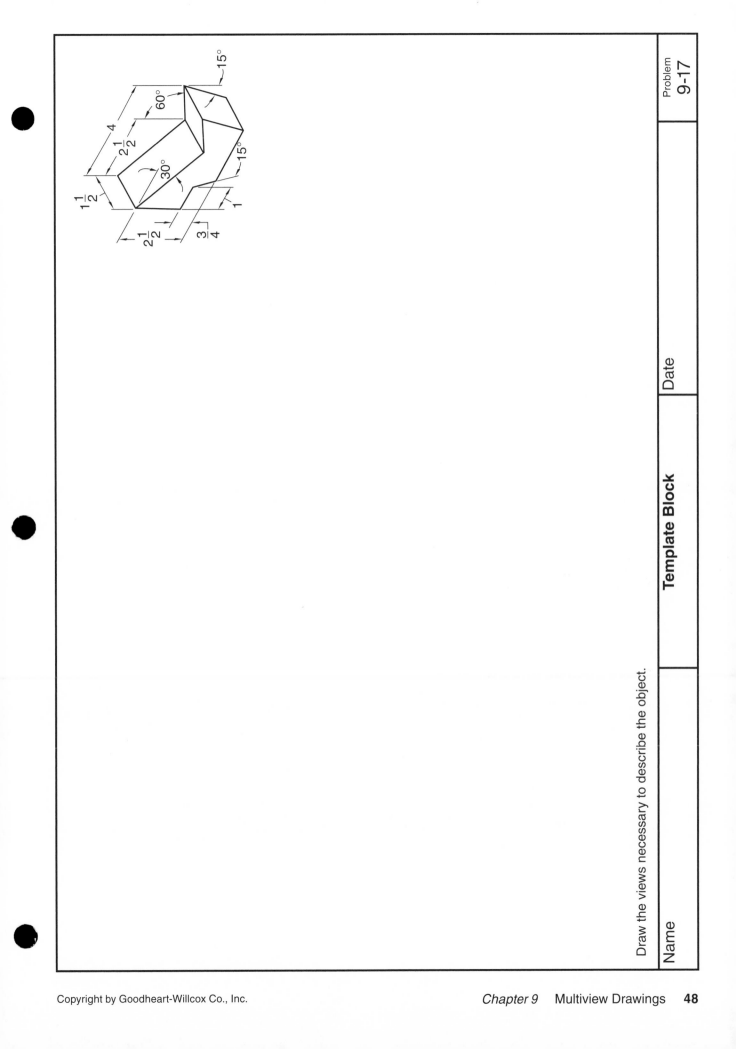

Draw the views necessary to describe the object.

Name

Template Block

Date

2× ∅.875

R1.25

1.5

1.5 DEEP

Draw the views necessary to describe the object.

Name	Link	Date
		Problem 9-18

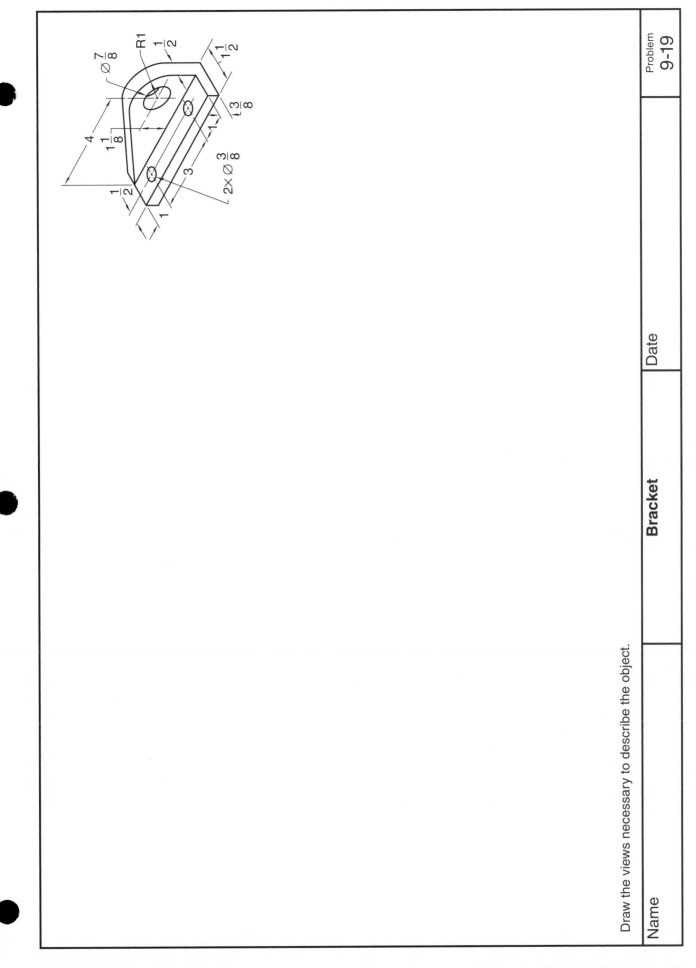

Draw the views necessary to describe the object.

Bracket

Name

Date

4X Ø.312
EQ SP

.75
Ø4.75
Ø4.25

1

Ø3.5

Ø1.25

Ø2.0

Draw the views necessary to describe the object.

Name

Flange

Date

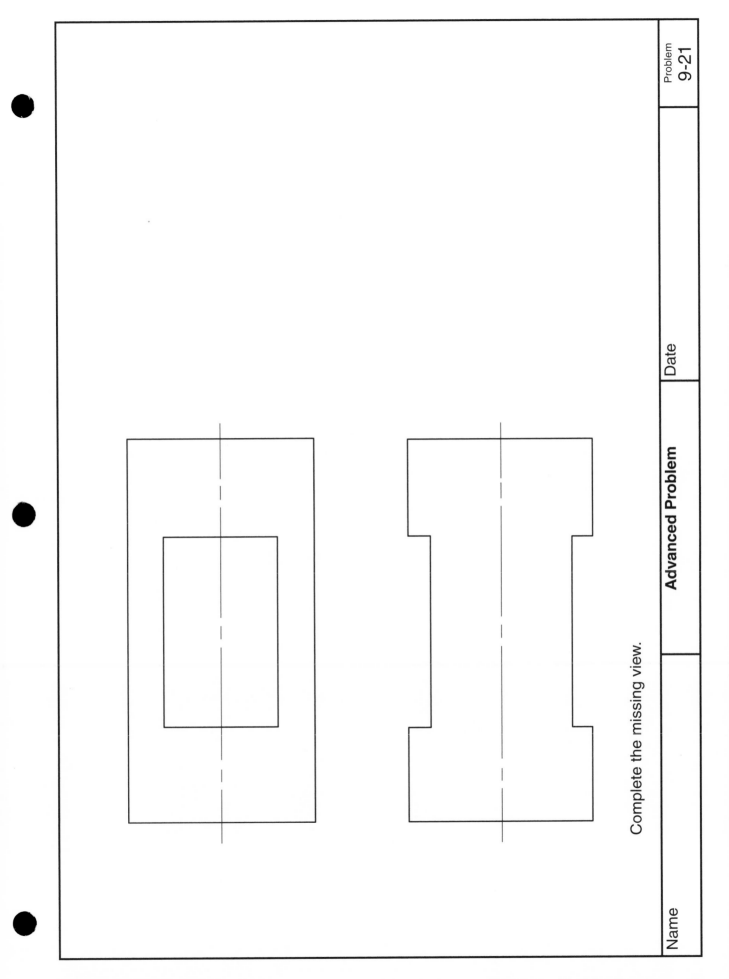

Complete the missing view.

Name

Advanced Problem

Date

Problem
9-21

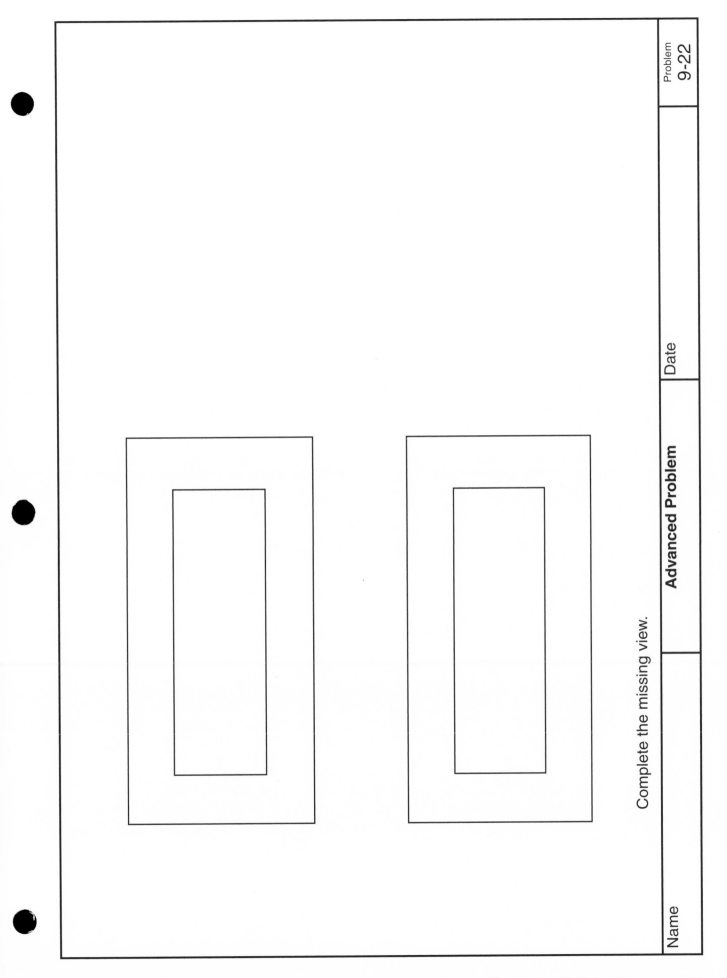

Complete the missing view.

Date

Advanced Problem

Name

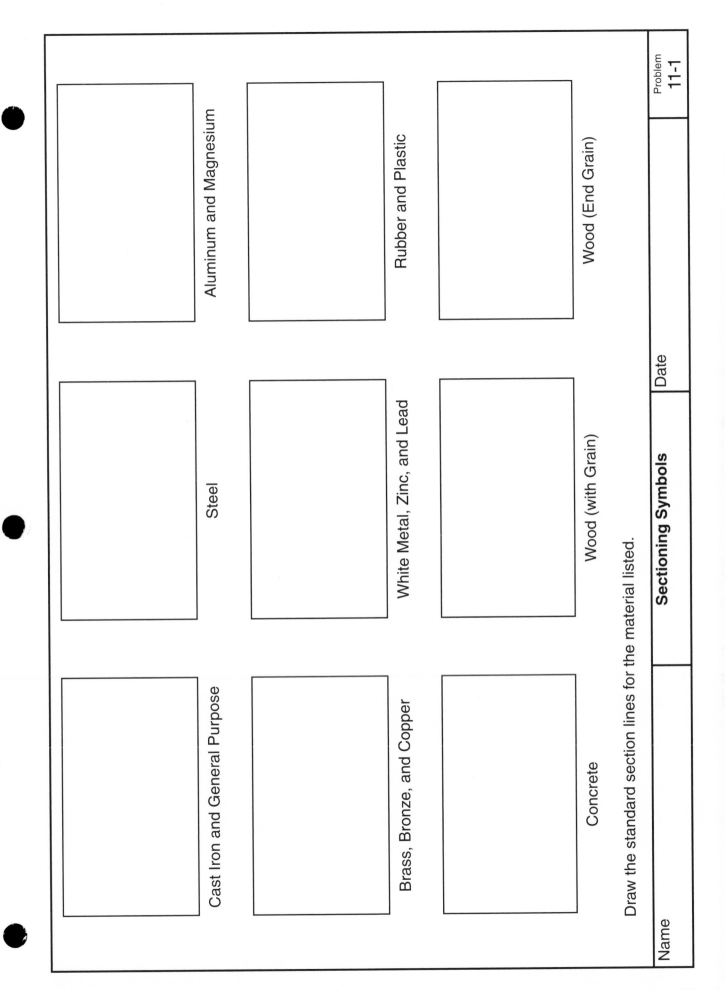

Aluminum and Magnesium

Rubber and Plastic

Wood (End Grain)

Steel

White Metal, Zinc, and Lead

Wood (with Grain)

Cast Iron and General Purpose

Brass, Bronze, and Copper

Concrete

Draw the standard section lines for the material listed.

Sectioning Symbols

Name

Date

Problem
11-1

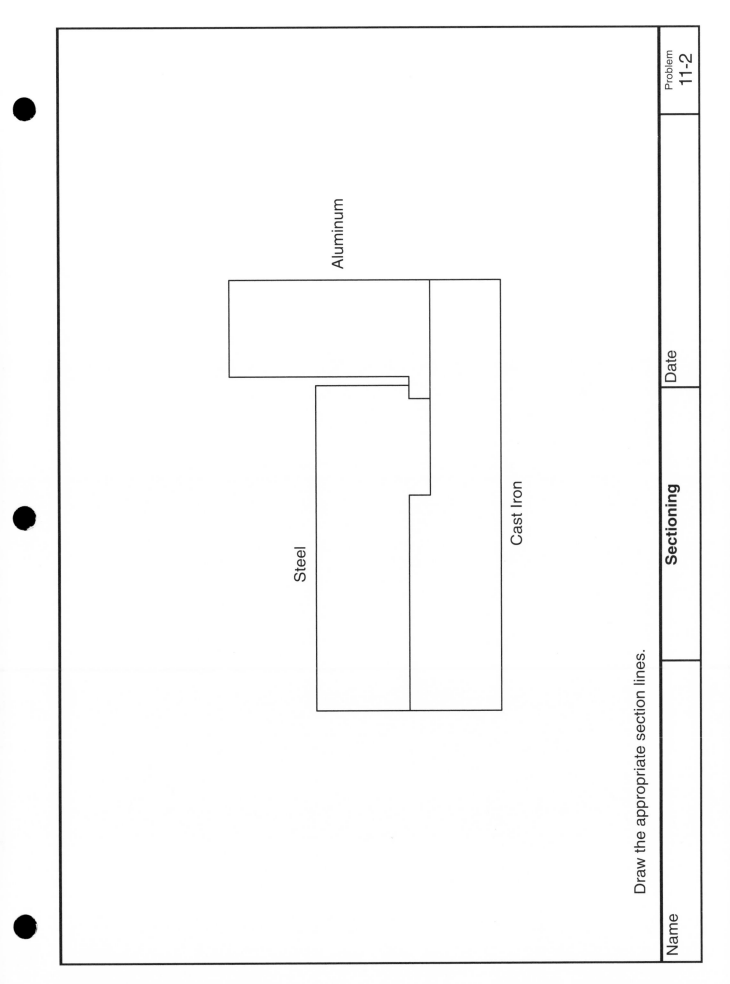

Aluminum

Steel

Cast Iron

Draw the appropriate section lines.

| Name | | Sectioning | Date | Problem 11-2 |

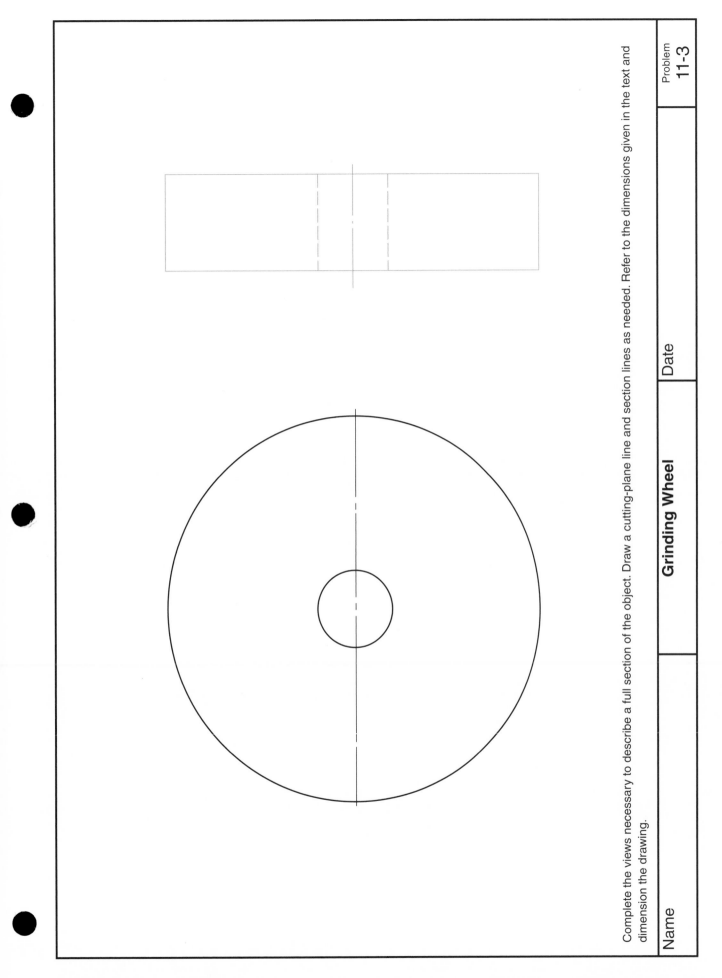

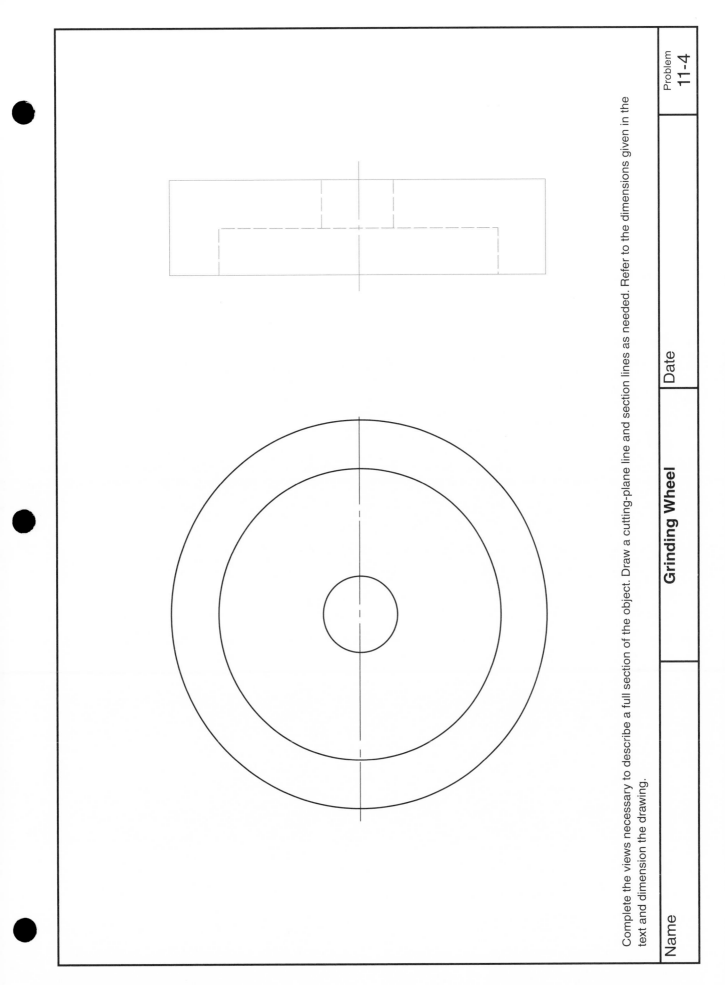

Complete the views necessary to describe a full section of the object. Draw a cutting-plane line and section lines as needed. Refer to the dimensions given in the text and dimension the drawing.

Grinding Wheel

Name

Date

Problem
11-4

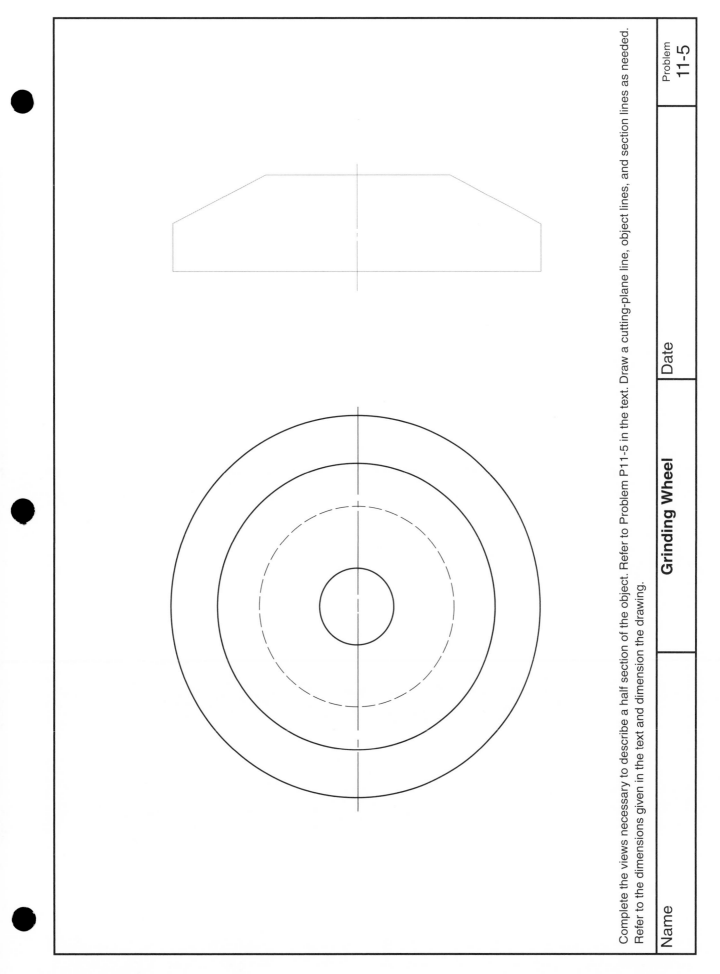

Complete the views necessary to describe a half section of the object. Refer to Problem P11-5 in the text. Draw a cutting-plane line, object lines, and section lines as needed. Refer to the dimensions given in the text and dimension the drawing.

Grinding Wheel

Name

Date

Problem
11-5

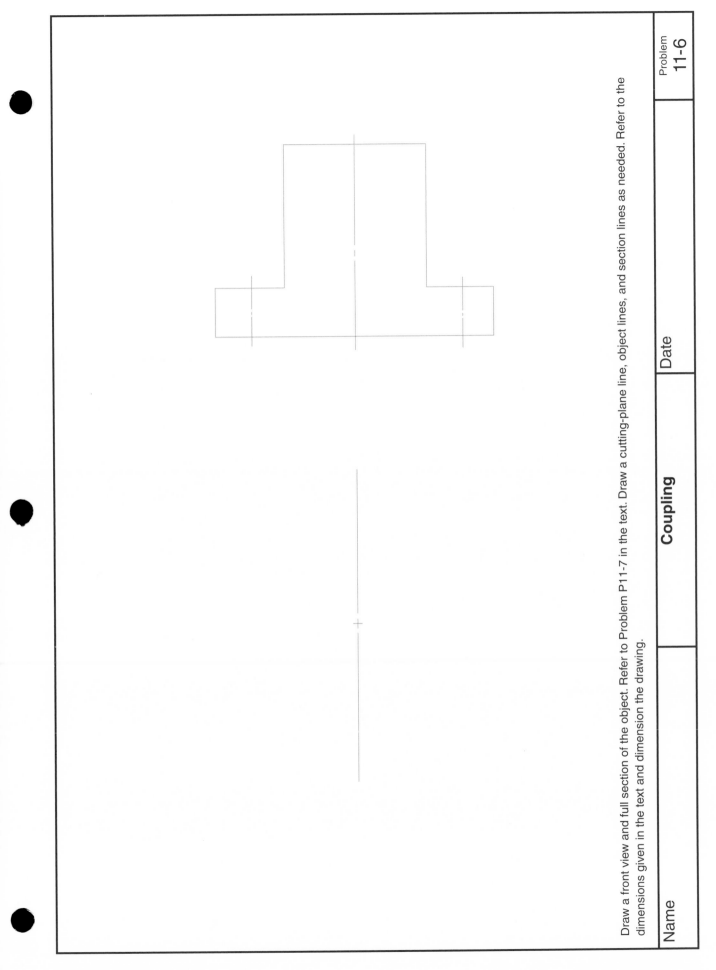

Draw a front view and full section of the object. Refer to Problem P11-7 in the text. Draw a cutting-plane line, object lines, and section lines as needed. Refer to the dimensions given in the text and dimension the drawing.

Date

Coupling

Name

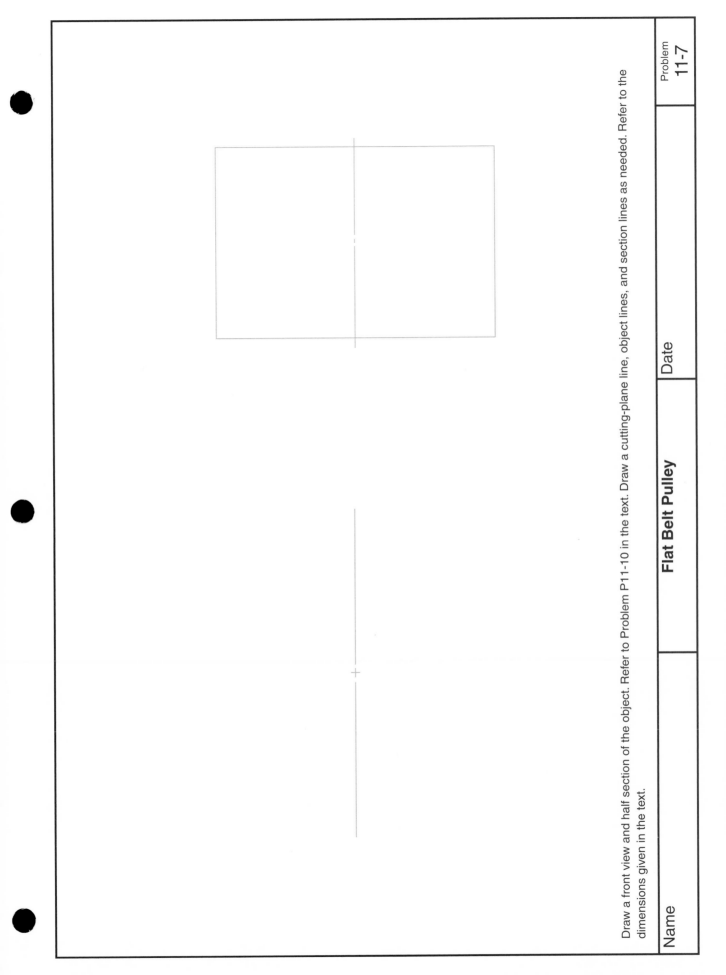

Draw a front view and half section of the object. Refer to Problem P11-10 in the text. Draw a cutting-plane line, object lines, and section lines as needed. Refer to the dimensions given in the text.

| Name | | Flat Belt Pulley | Date | Problem 11-7 |

Draw the views needed to show the shape of the spacer. Draw the right-side view as an offset section through the three holes. Draw the cutting-plane line on the primary view and dimension the drawing.

Name		Date
	Spacer	Problem **11-8**

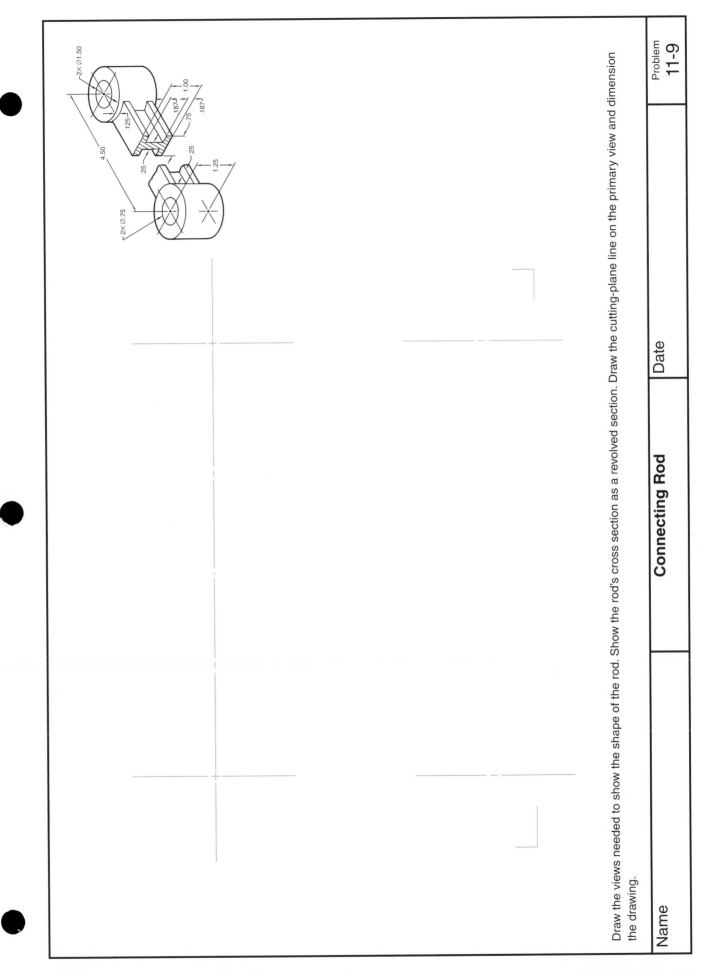

Draw the views needed to show the shape of the rod. Show the rod's cross section as a revolved section. Draw the cutting-plane line on the primary view and dimension the drawing.

Name			Date		Problem 11-9
	Connecting Rod				

125 × .250 KEYWAY
Ø21.00 REAM
5X Ø2.50 DRILL
EQ SP
1.00
Ø3.00
Ø4.00

Draw the views needed to show the shape of the plate. Draw the right-side view as an aligned section and dimension the drawing.

Adapter Plate

Name

Date

Problem
11-10

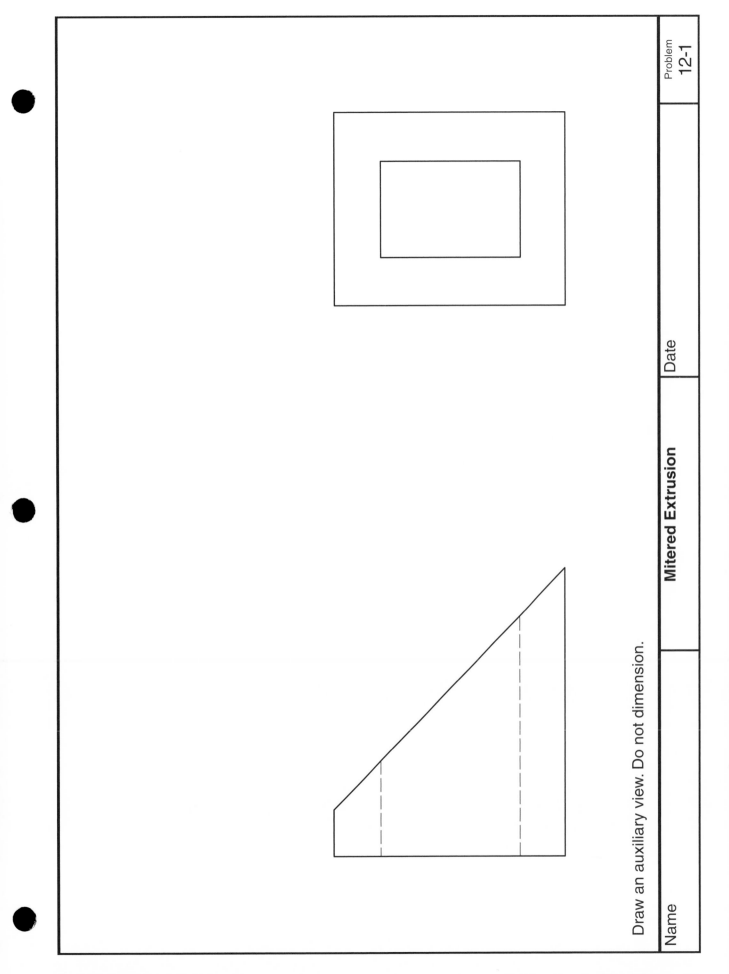

Draw an auxiliary view. Do not dimension.

Mitered Extrusion

Problem 12-1

Name

Date

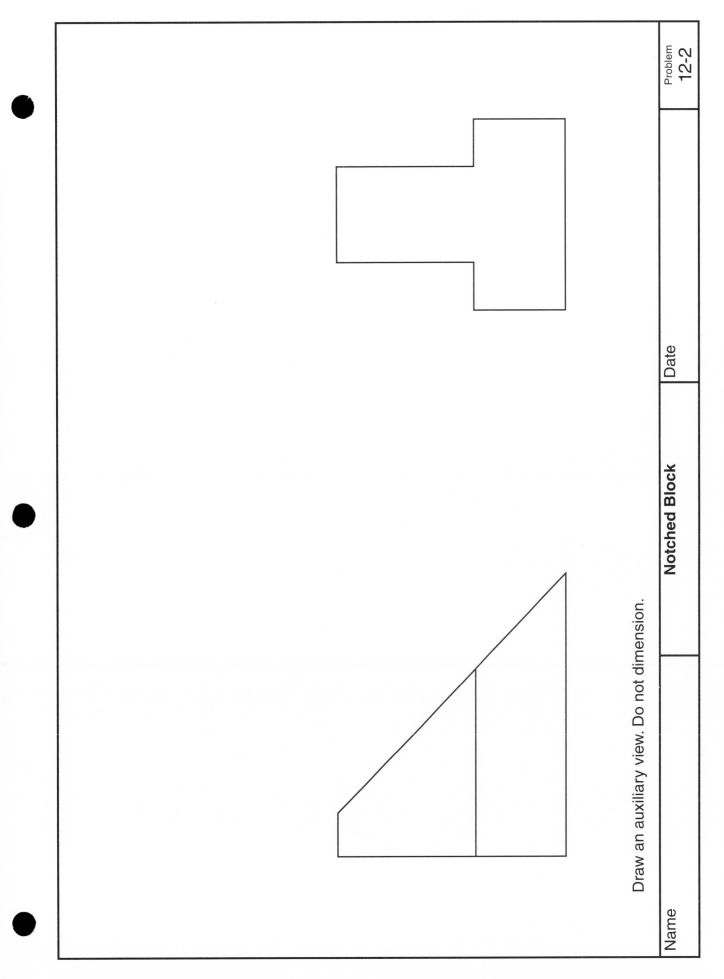

Draw an auxiliary view. Do not dimension.

Name

Notched Block

Date

Problem
12-2

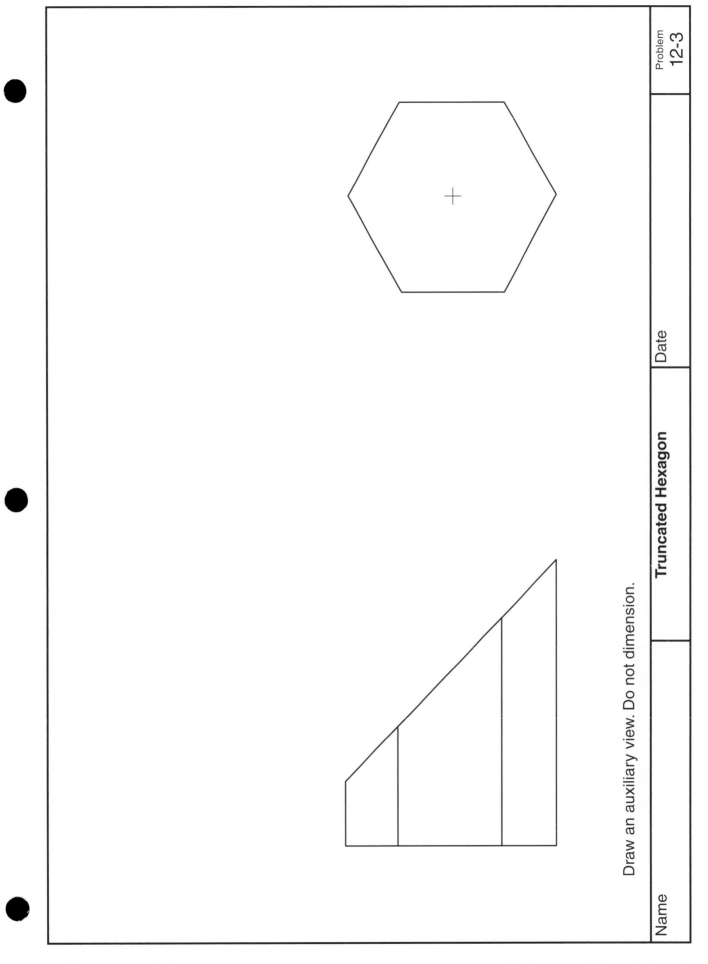

Draw an auxiliary view. Do not dimension.

Truncated Hexagon

Date

Name

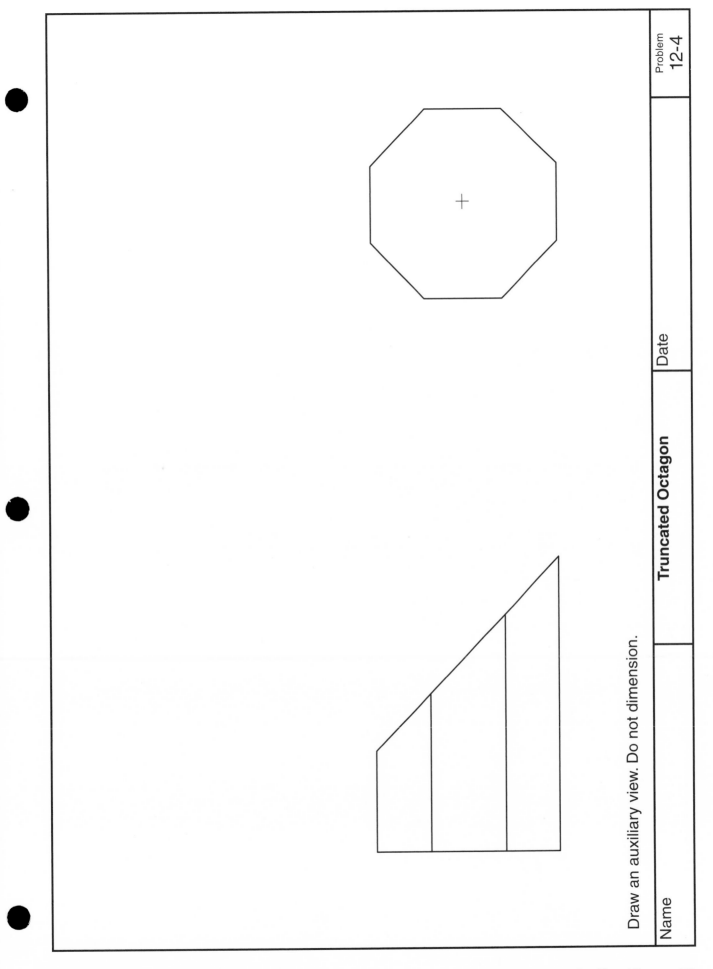

Draw an auxiliary view. Do not dimension.

Name		Date	Problem
	Truncated Octagon		12-4

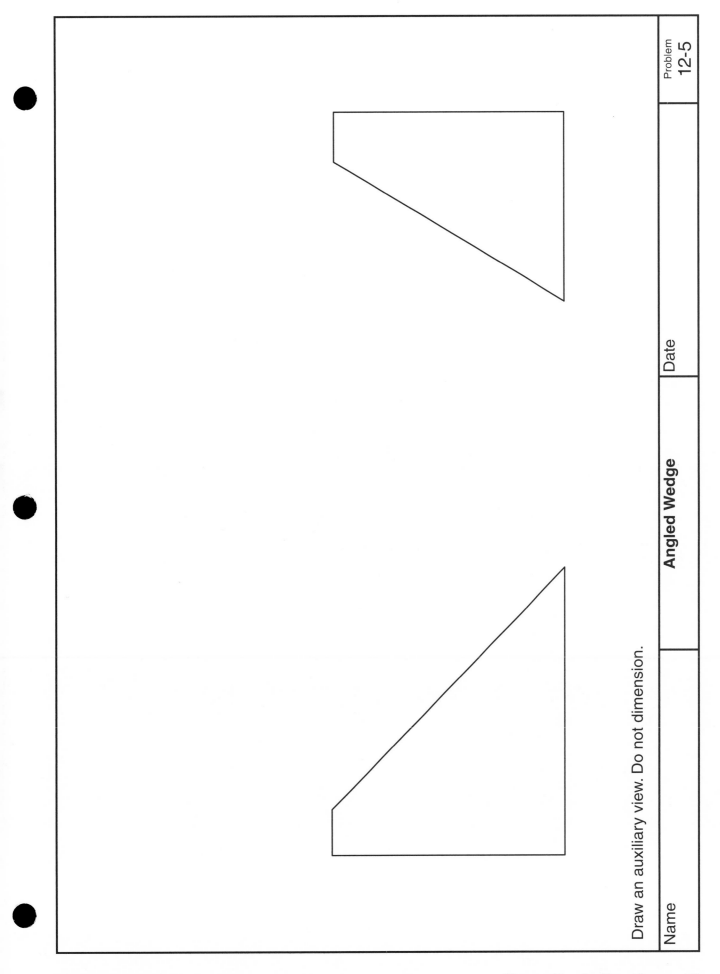

Draw an auxiliary view. Do not dimension.

Name

Date

Angled Wedge

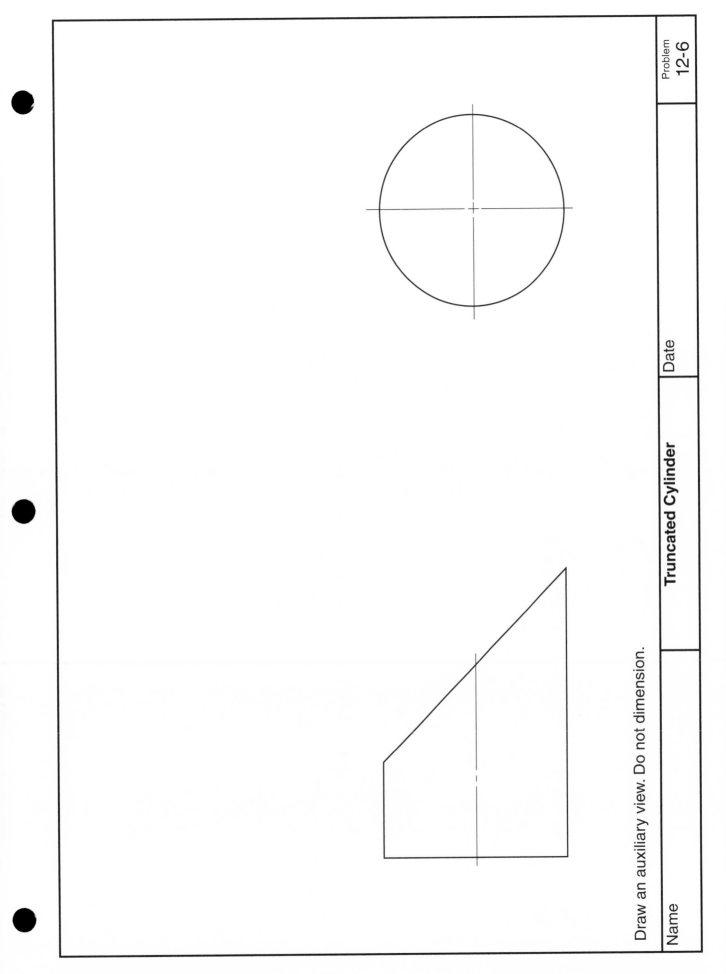

Draw an auxiliary view. Do not dimension.

Truncated Cylinder

Problem
12-6

Date

Name

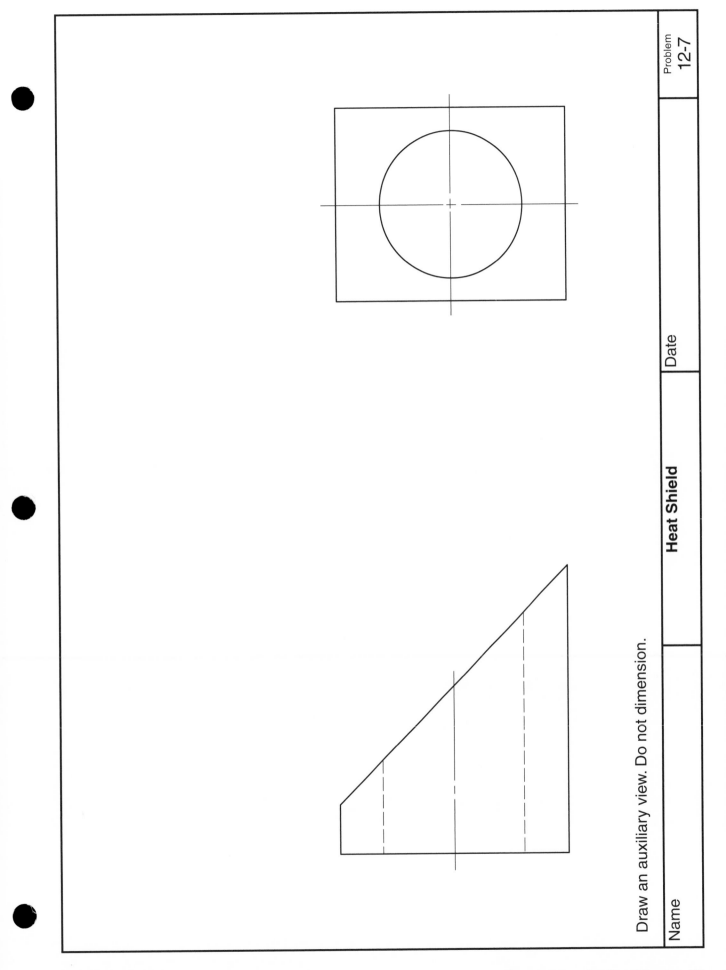

Draw an auxiliary view. Do not dimension.

Name	Heat Shield	Date

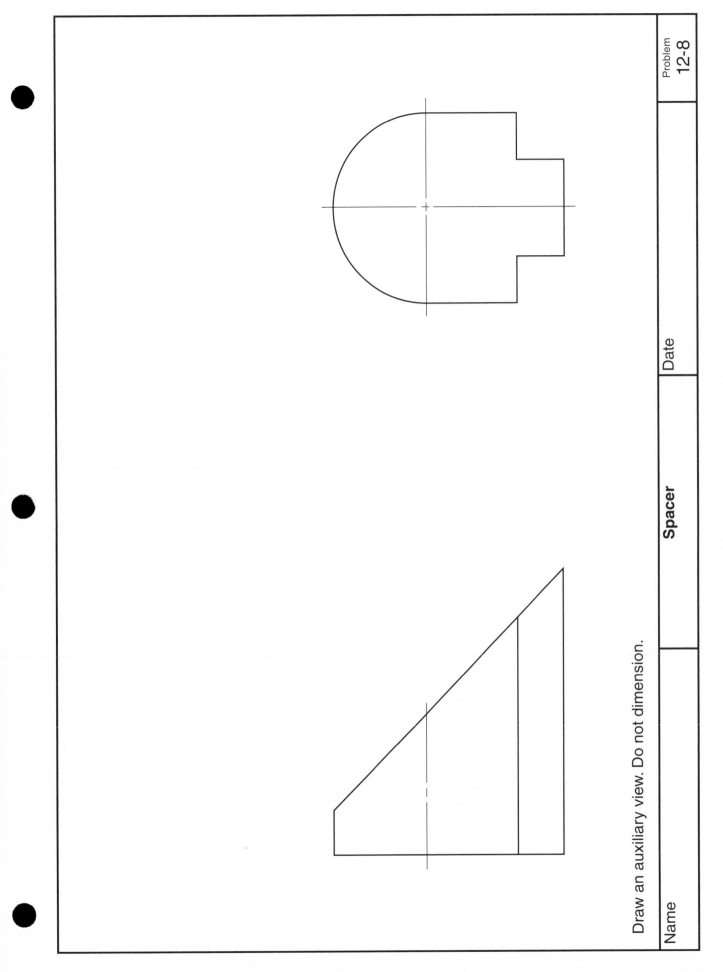

Draw an auxiliary view. Do not dimension.

Spacer

Date

Name

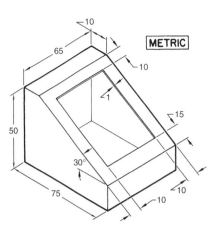

METRIC

Draw the orthographic and auxiliary
views needed to describe the object.
Do not dimension.

Name	**Instrument Case**	Date	Problem 12-9

Draw the orthographic and auxiliary views needed to describe the object. Do not dimension.

$R\frac{3}{4}$

$2\times\varnothing\frac{1}{2}$

$\frac{15}{16}$

$\frac{15}{16}$

$2\frac{7}{16}$

$30°$

$\frac{3}{8}\times 45°$

$\frac{3}{4}$

$\frac{1}{8}$

$\frac{1}{2}$

$\frac{3}{8}$

$\frac{3}{16}$

Name

Bracket

Date

Draw the orthographic and auxiliary views needed to describe the object. Do not dimension.

2X Ø.75

.75
1.5
.75
1.5
1.0
.5
.5
1.0
1.5
.75
.75
.37
.37
45°
.75
.187

Name

Hanger Clamp

Date

Problem
12-11

Copyright by Goodheart-Willcox Co., Inc.

Chapter 12   Auxiliary Views   **80**

Draw the orthographic and auxiliary views needed to describe the object. Do not dimension.

.25
1.50
.50
1.00
Ø.437 THRU
Ø1.00
.50
.50
45°
.62
3.00

Name

Date

Shifter Bar

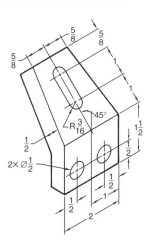

Draw the orthographic and
auxiliary views needed to
describe the object.
Do not dimension.

Name	**Support**	Date	Problem 12-13

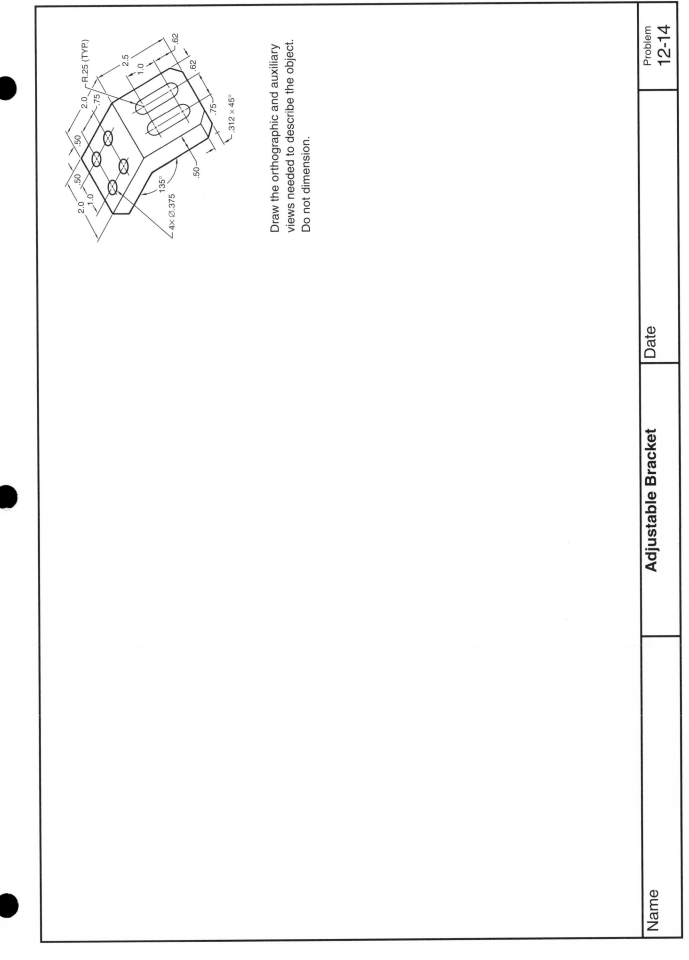

Draw the orthographic and auxiliary views needed to describe the object. Do not dimension.

R.25 (TYP.)
2.5
1.0
.62
2.0
.75
.62
.50
.75
.50
.312 × 45°
2.0
135°
.50
1.0
4× Ø.375

Name

Adjustable Bracket

Date

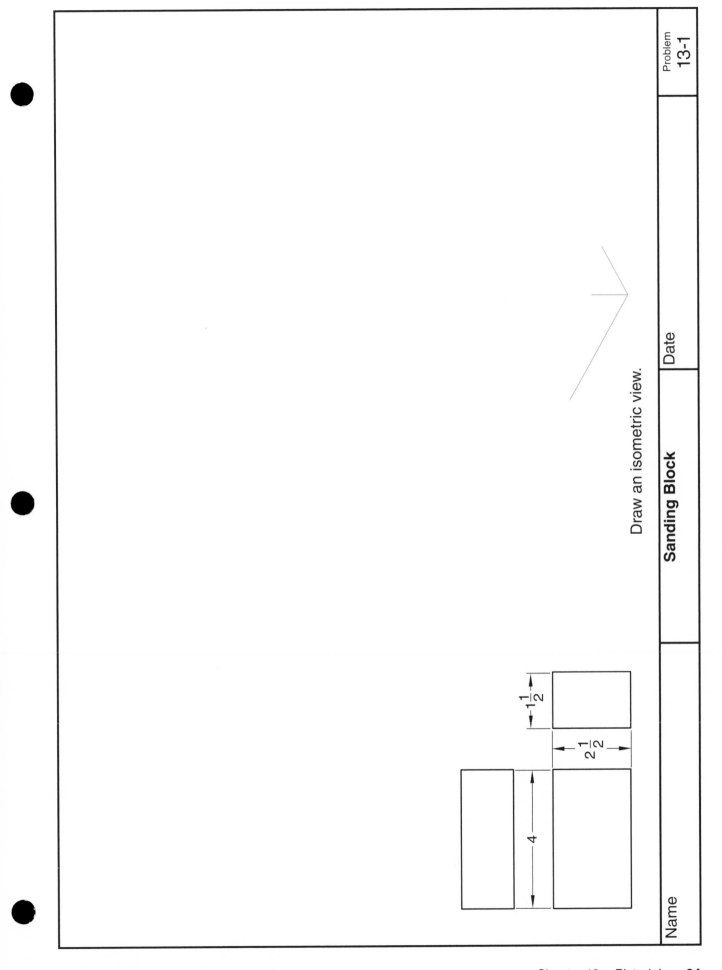

Draw an isometric view.

$1\frac{1}{2}$

$2\frac{1}{2}$

4

Copyright by Goodheart-Willcox Co., Inc.

Name

Date

Sanding Block

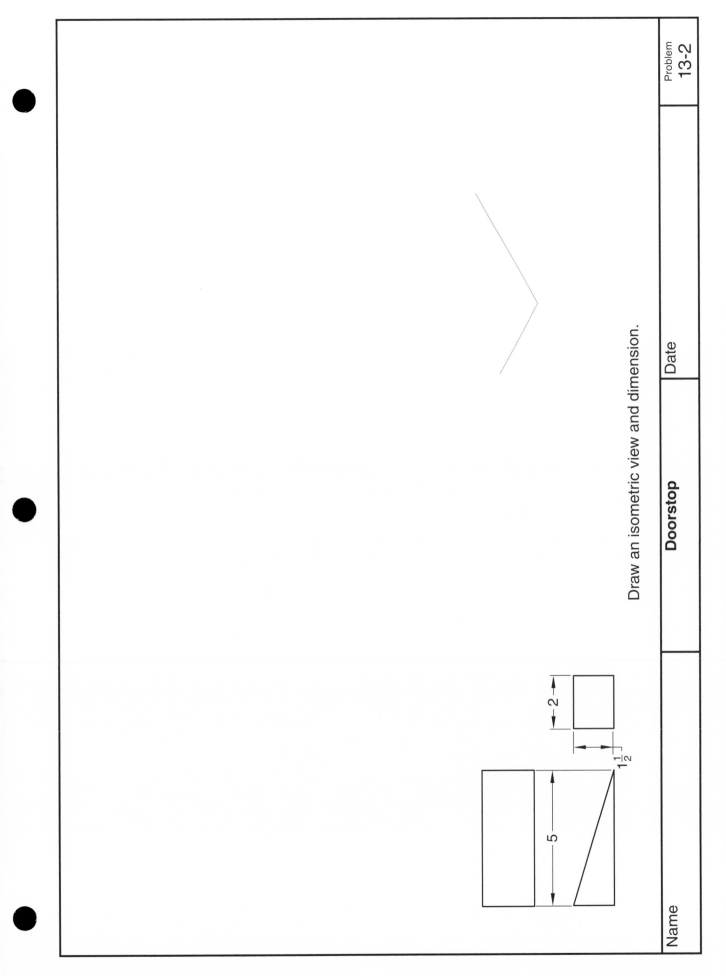

Draw an isometric view and dimension.

Doorstop

2

1½

5

Name

Date

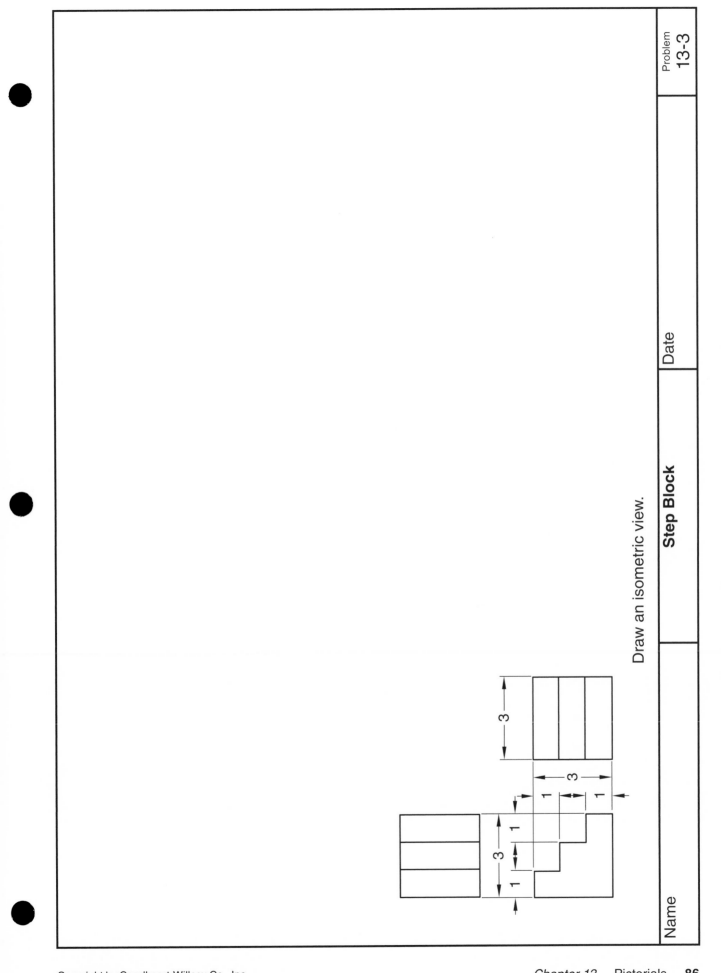

Draw an isometric view.

Name		Step Block	Date	Problem 13-3

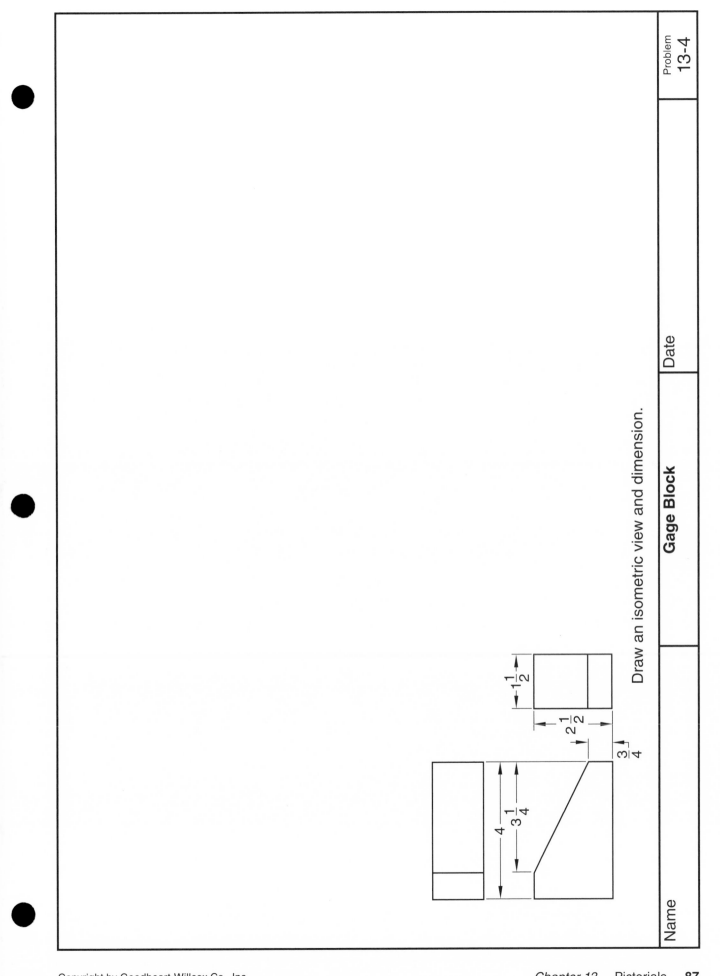

Draw an isometric view and dimension.

Name

Gage Block

Date

$1\frac{1}{2}$

$2\frac{1}{2}$

$\frac{3}{4}$

4

$3\frac{1}{4}$

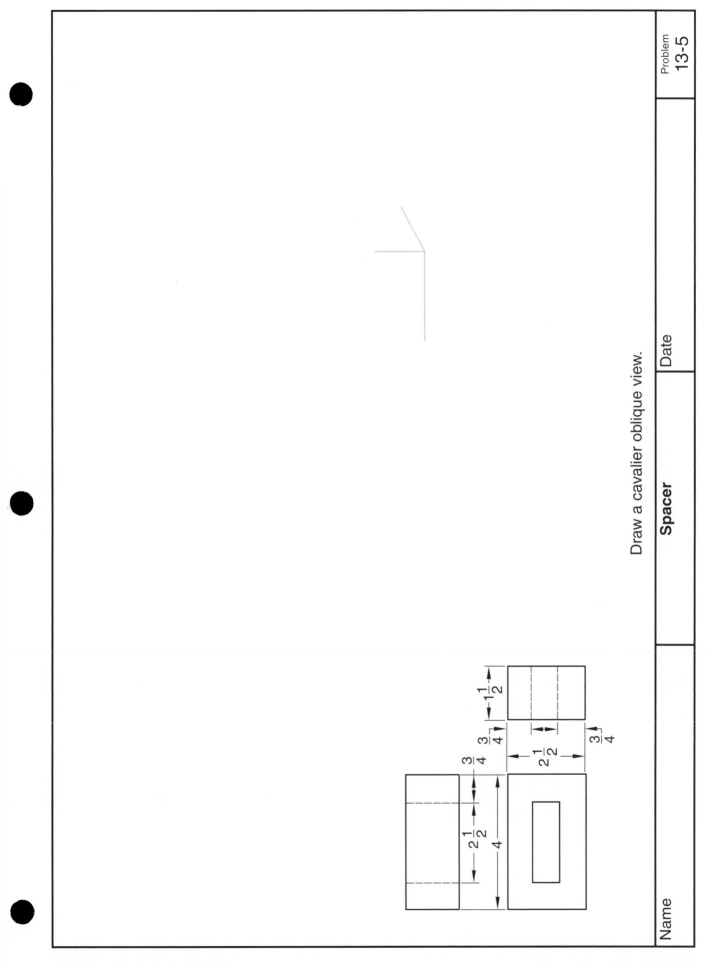

Draw a cavalier oblique view.

Spacer

$1\frac{1}{2}$

$\frac{3}{4}$

$\frac{3}{4}$

$2\frac{1}{2}$

$\frac{3}{4}$

$\frac{3}{4}$

$2\frac{1}{2}$

4

Date

Name

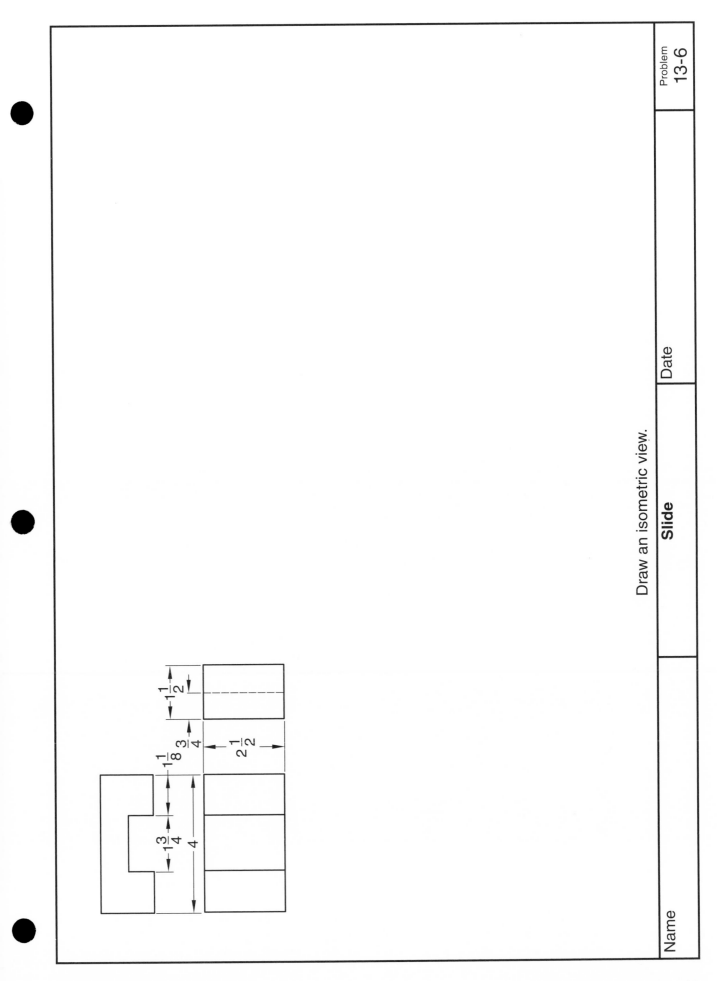

Draw an isometric view.

Name   Slide   Date

Problem
13-6

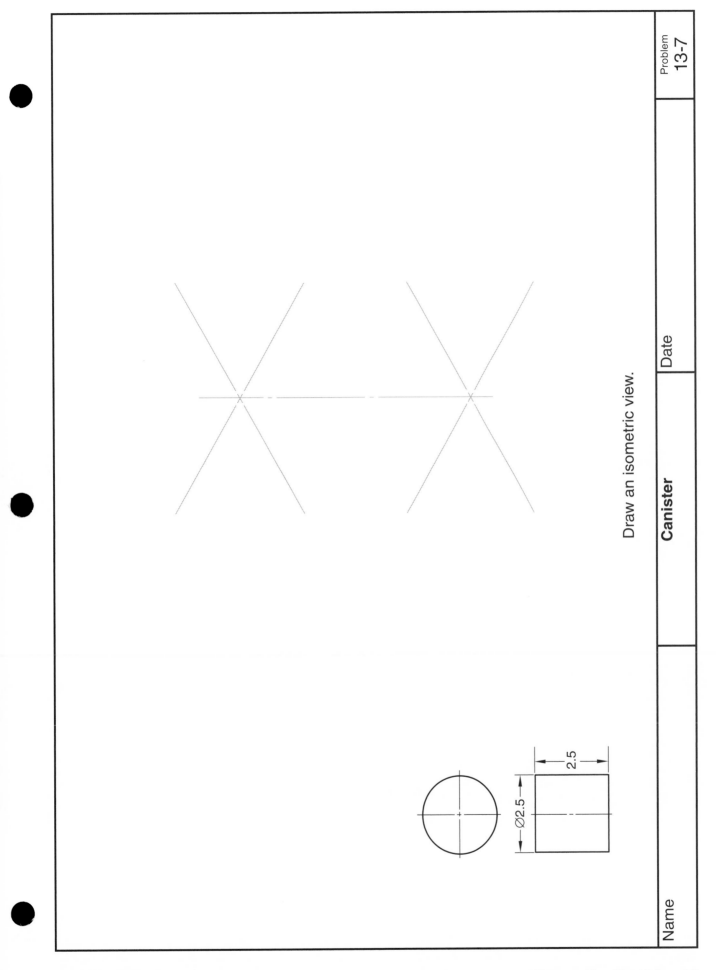

Draw an isometric view.

Canister

Ø2.5

2.5

Date

Name

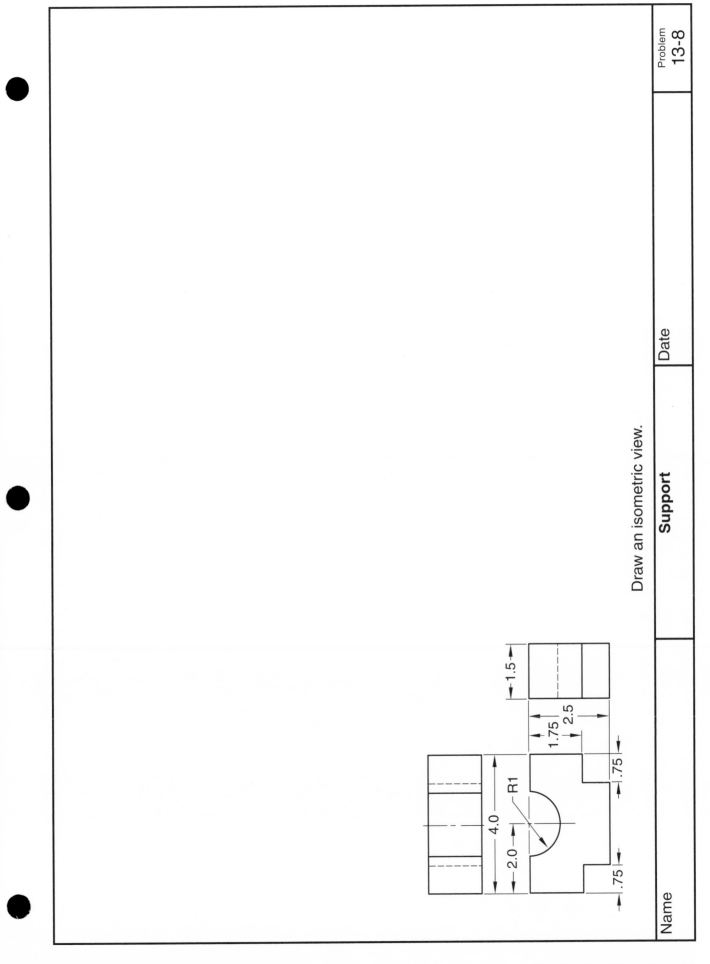

Draw an isometric view.

Name

Support

Date

Problem
13-8

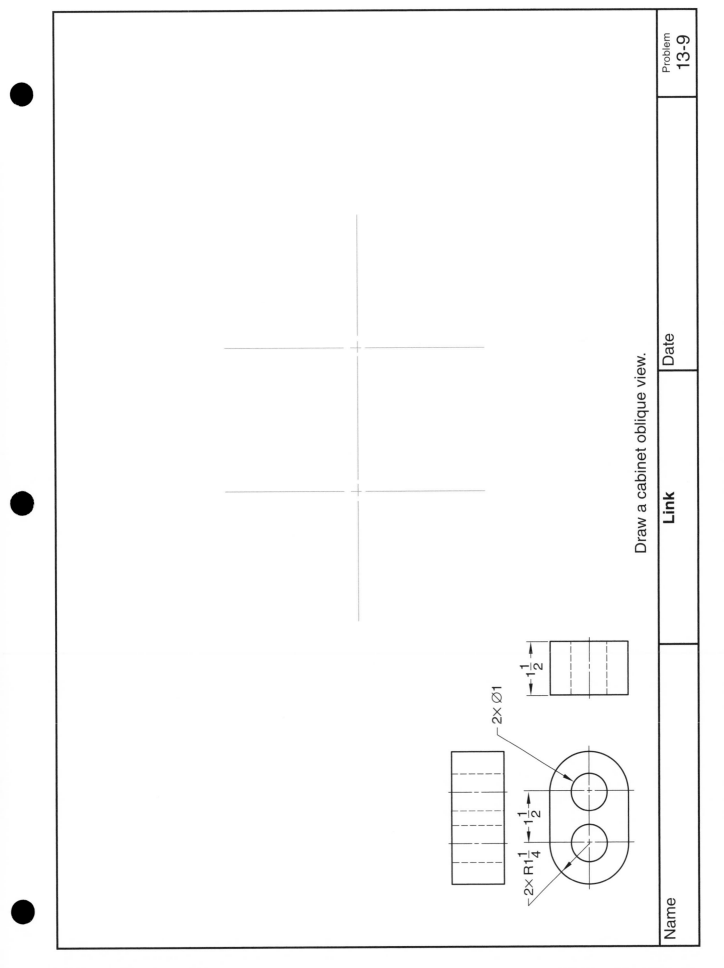

Draw a cabinet oblique view.

$1\frac{1}{2}$

$2\times \varnothing 1$

$1\frac{1}{2}$

$2\times R1\frac{1}{4}$

Name

Link   Date

Problem
13-9

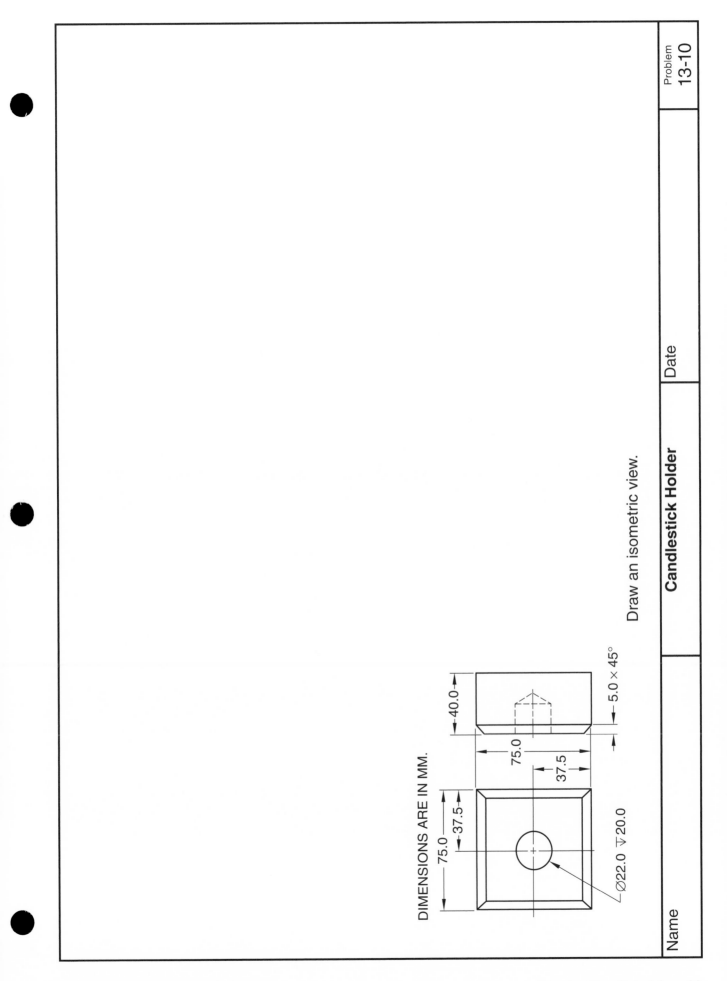

DIMENSIONS ARE IN MM.

40.0

75.0

37.5

Ø22.0 ⊽ 20.0

75.0

37.5

5.0 × 45°

Draw an isometric view.

Date

Candlestick Holder

Name

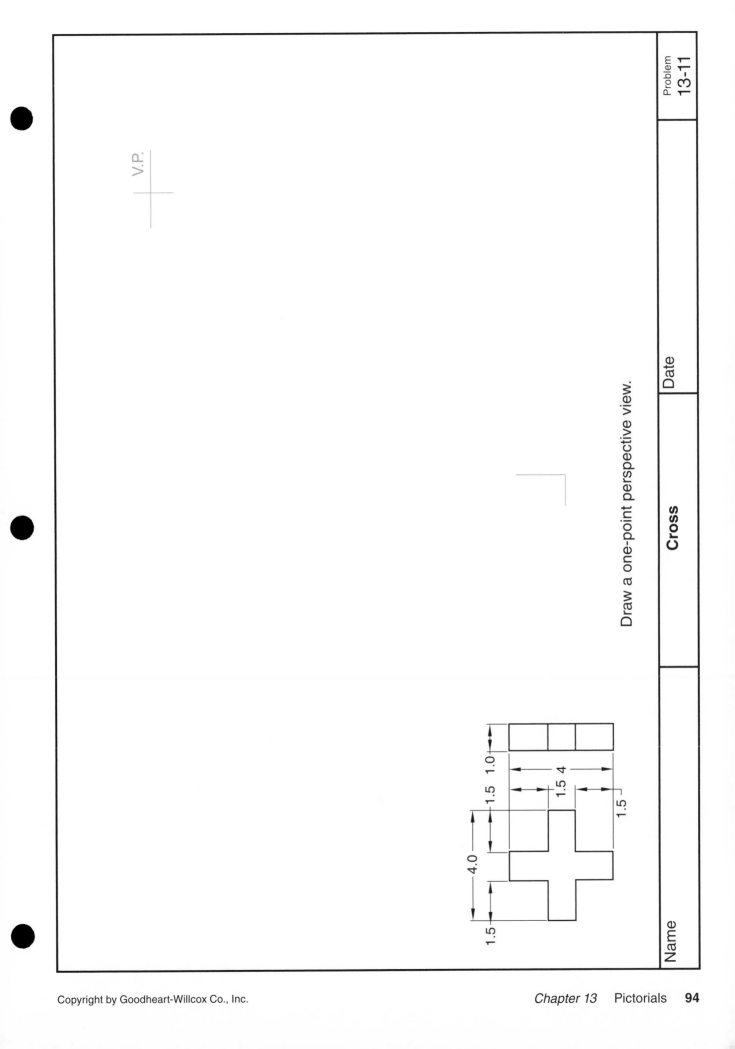

V.P.

Draw a one-point perspective view.

Name

Cross

Date

Problem
13-11

Chapter 13   Pictorials   **94**

1.5

1.0

1.5   4

1.5

1.5

4.0

1.5

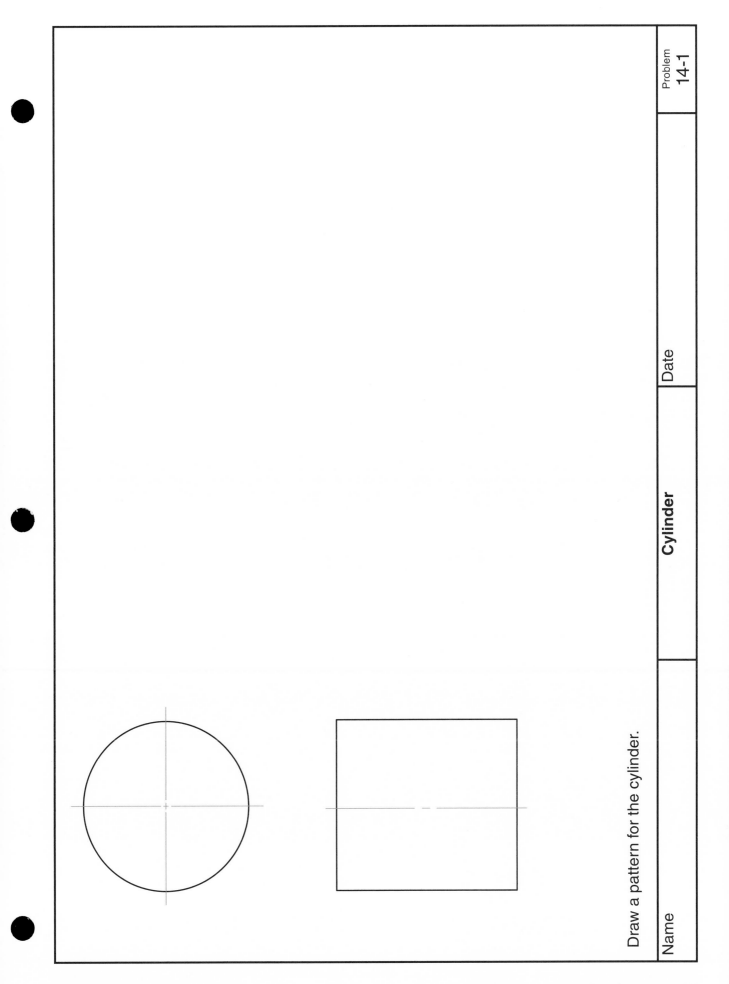

Draw a pattern for the cylinder.

Cylinder

Problem

14-1

Date

Name

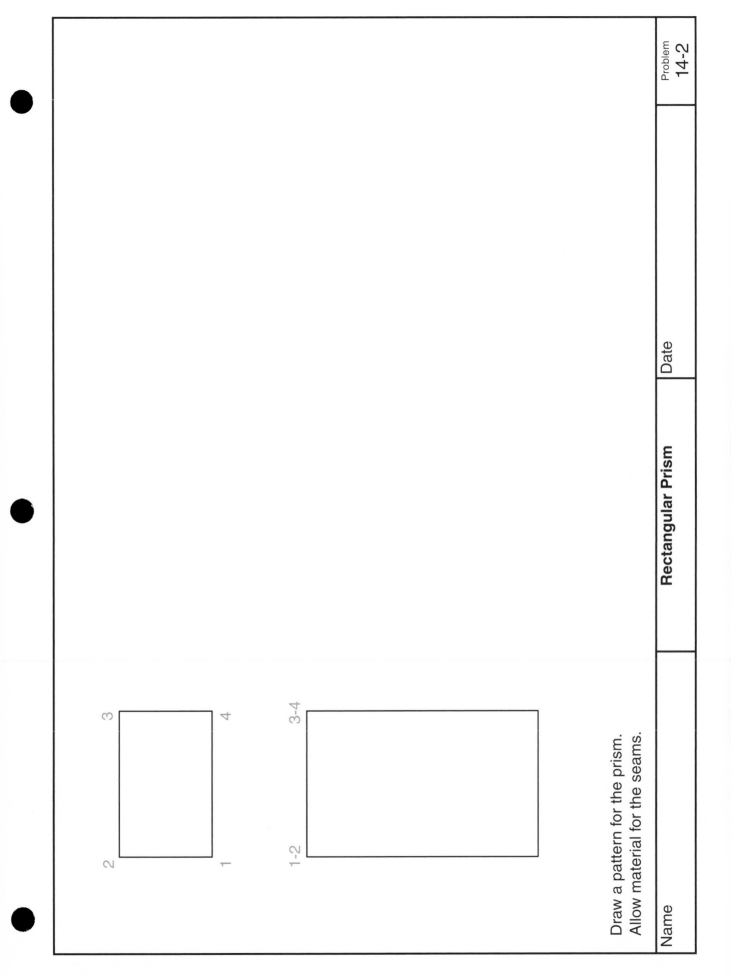

Draw a pattern for the prism.
Allow material for the seams.

Name

Rectangular Prism

Date

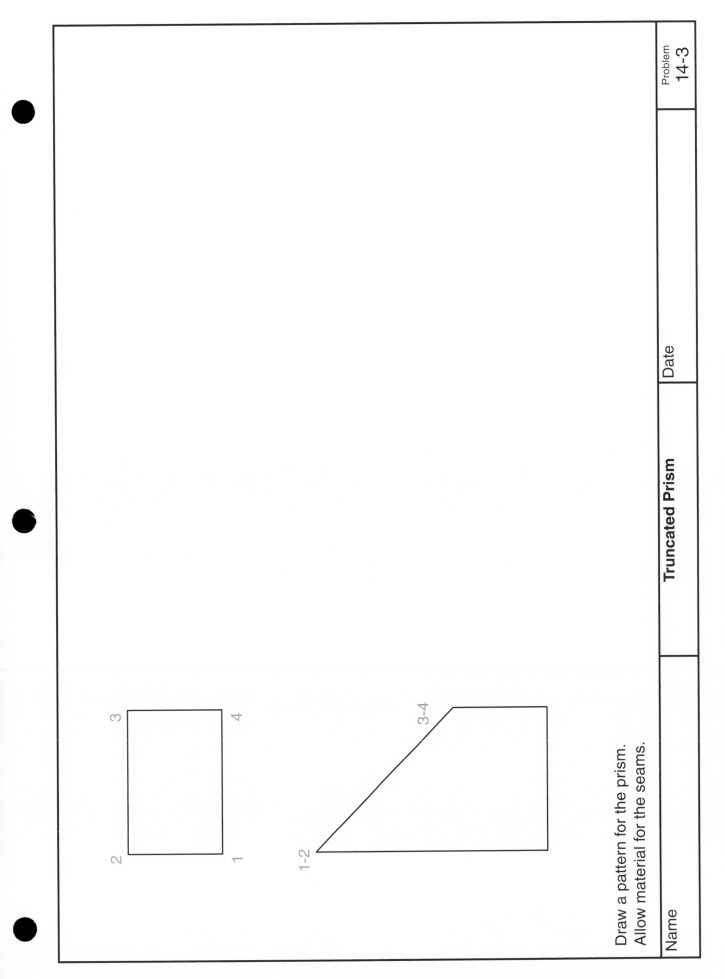

Draw a pattern for the prism.
Allow material for the seams.

Truncated Prism

Name _____ Date _____

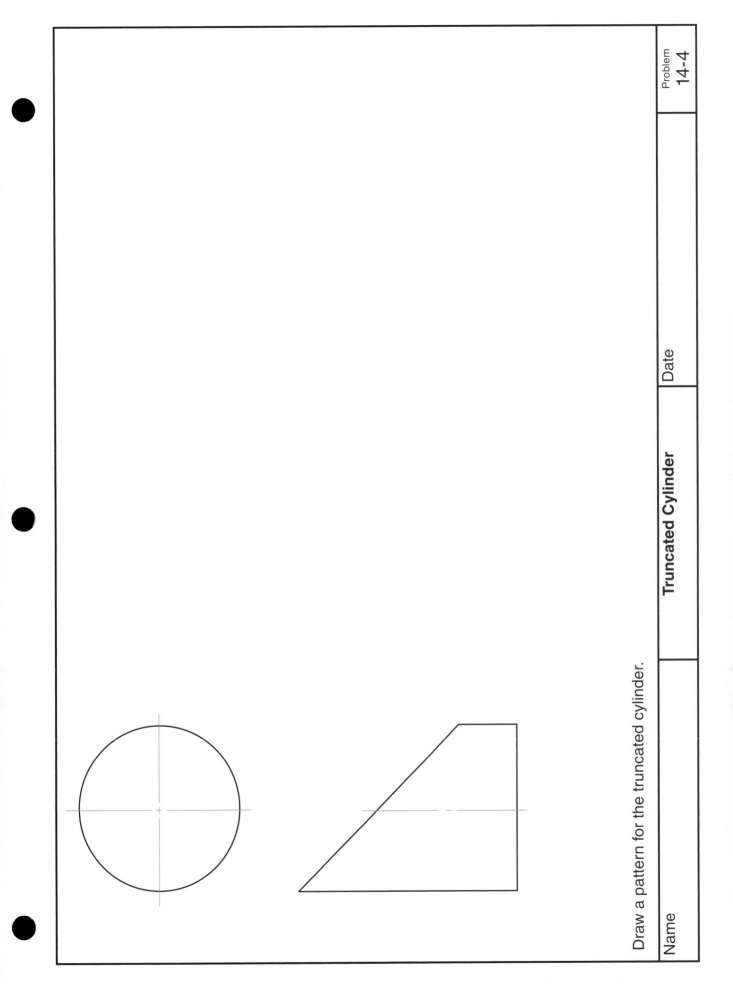

Draw a pattern for the truncated cylinder.

Truncated Cylinder

Name

Date

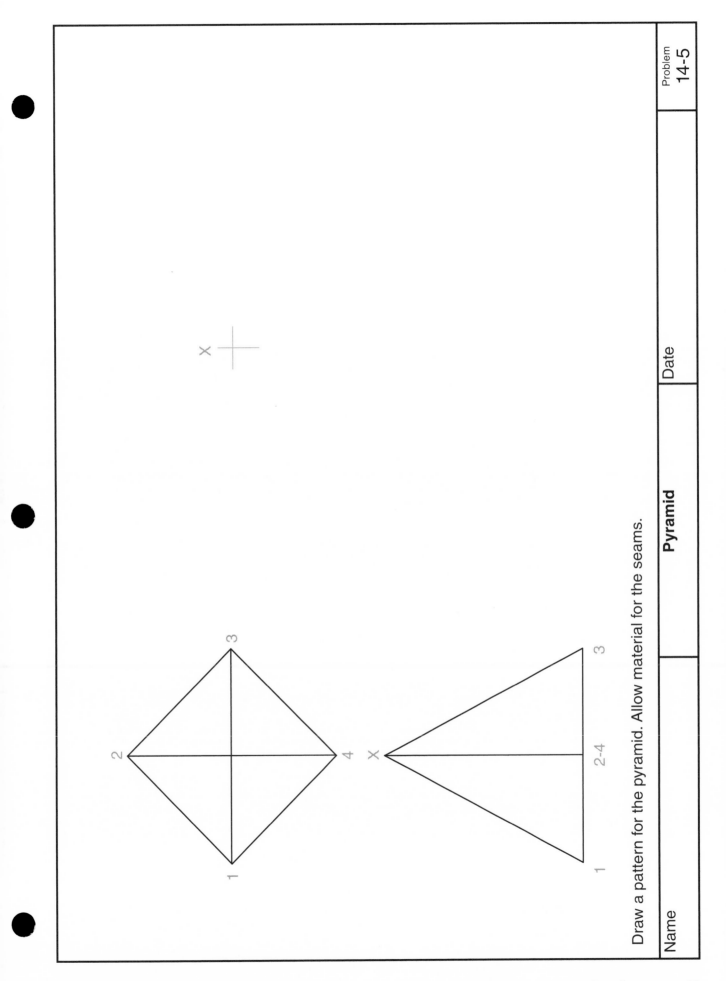

Draw a pattern for the pyramid. Allow material for the seams.

| Name | | Pyramid | Date |

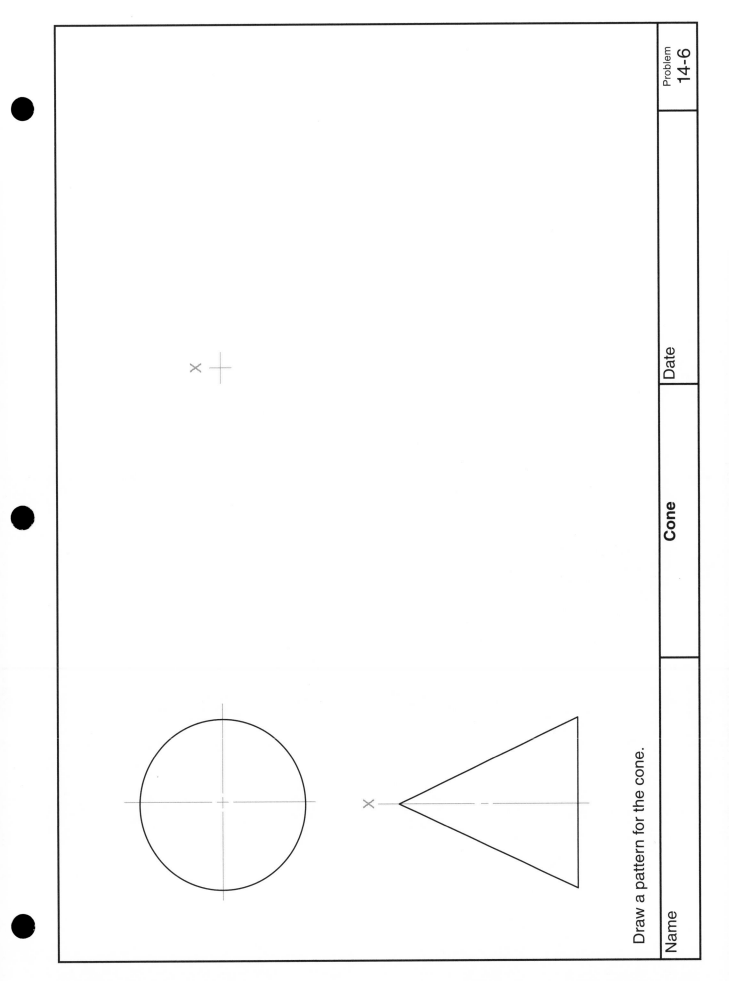

Draw a pattern for the cone.

Cone

Date

Name

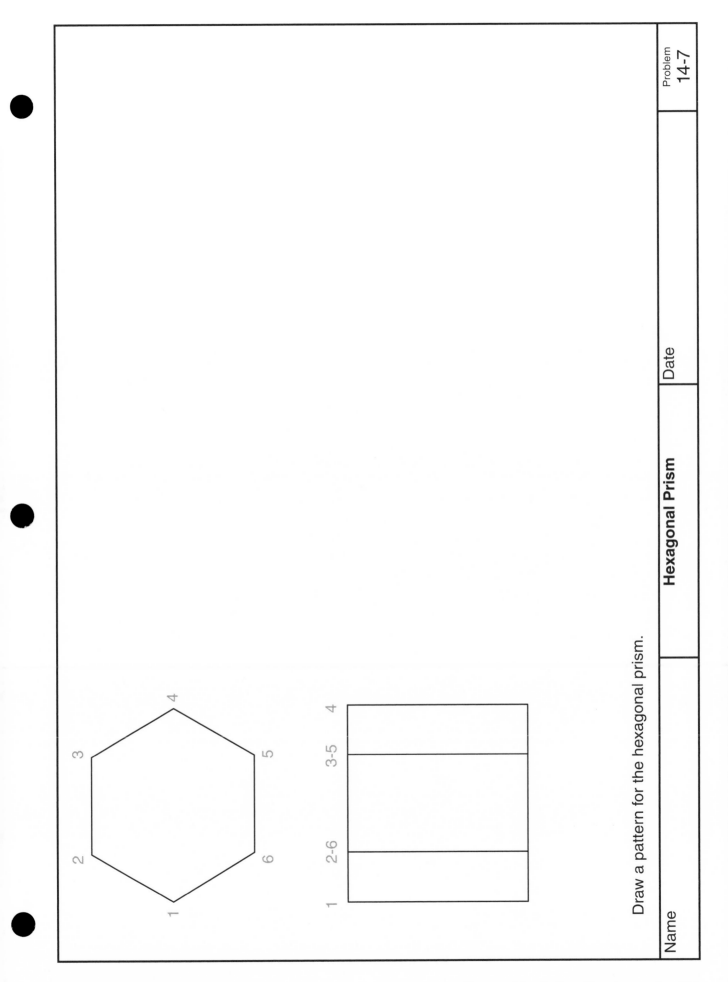

Draw a pattern for the hexagonal prism.

Hexagonal Prism

Problem 14-7

Name _____ Date _____

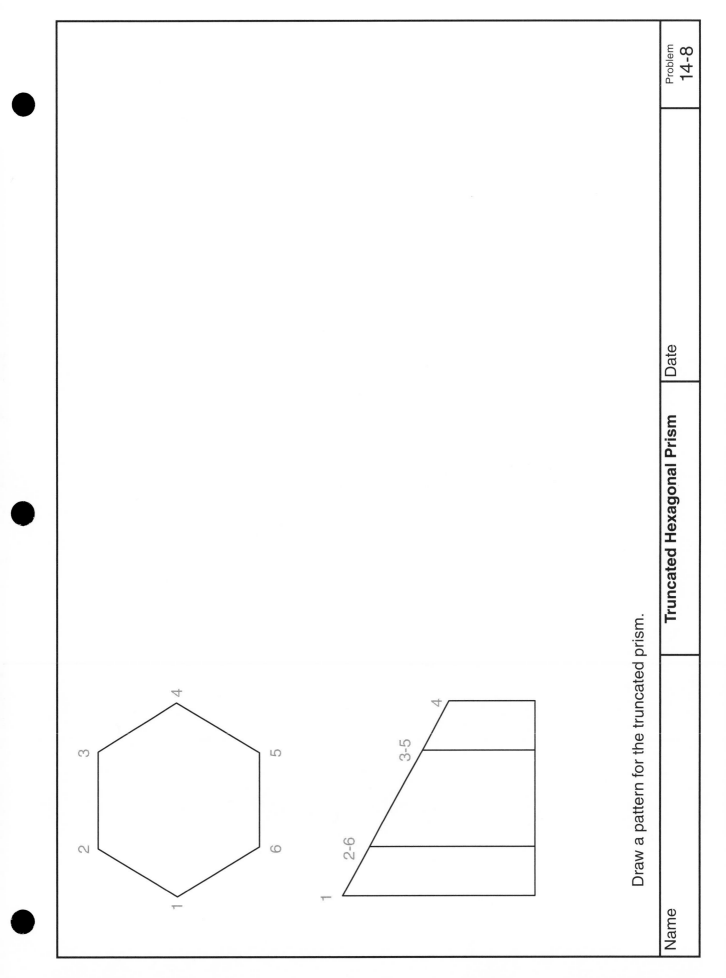

Draw a pattern for the truncated prism.

Name

Date

Truncated Hexagonal Prism

Refer to Problem 15-1 in the text and make a detail drawing of the machinist's square.

| Name | | Machinist's Square Details | Date | Problem 15-1 |

Refer to Problem 15-3 in the text and make an assembly drawing of the C-clamp.

C-Clamp Assembly

Name		Date

Refer to Problem 15-5 in the text and prepare a parts list and bill of materials for the deck gun.

Name		Date
Deck Gun Information		

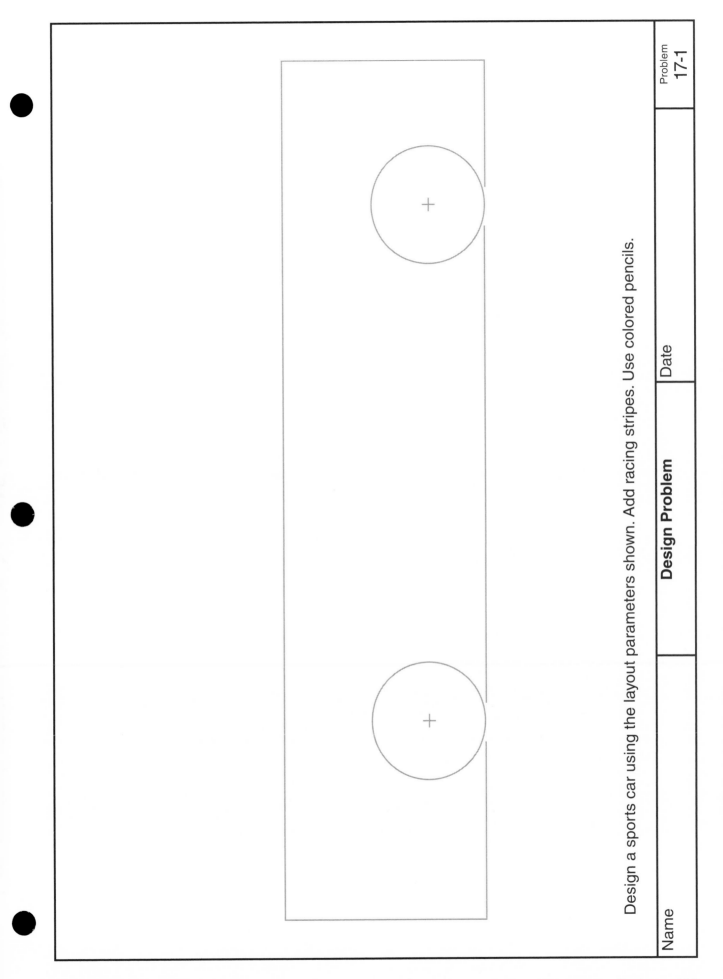

Design a sports car using the layout parameters shown. Add racing stripes. Use colored pencils.

Design Problem

Name

Date

Design a hand-launched glider in the space above. Construct a balsa model to verify flying characteristics.

| Name | Design Problem | Date | Problem 17-2 |

Draw a map of the school grounds at your school.

Name		School Grounds	Date

Draw a plot plan of the property on which your home is located.

Name		Date	
	Plot Plan		Problem
			19-2

Draw a map of your neighborhood.

Neighborhood Map

Name

Date

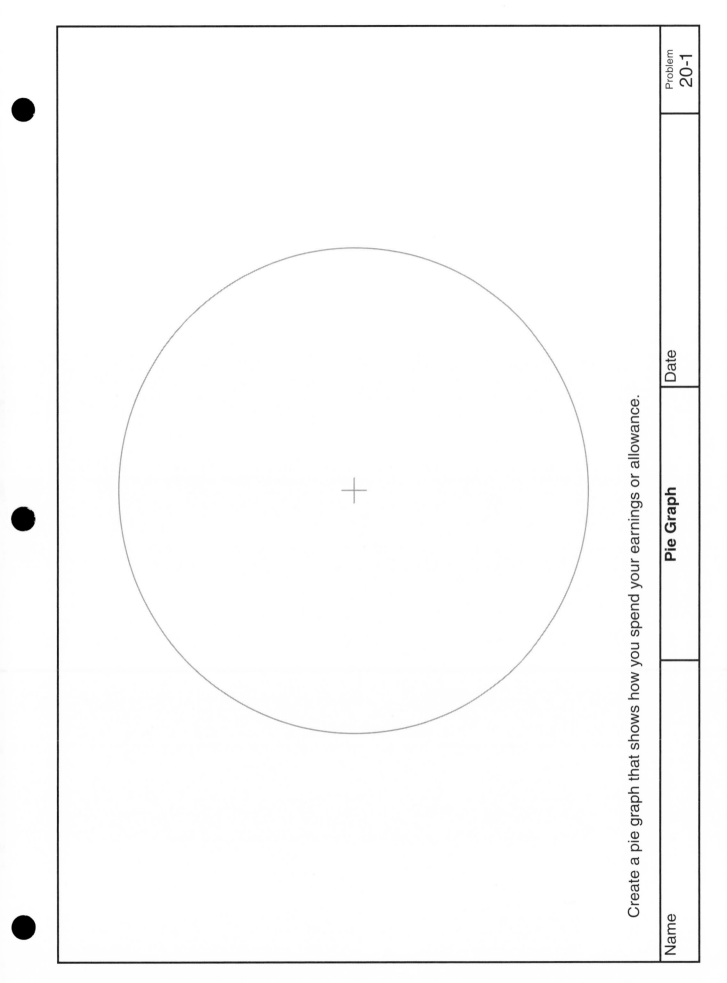

Create a pie graph that shows how you spend your earnings or allowance.

Pie Graph

Name

Date

Create a bar graph showing the change in automobile engine horsepower from 1940 to the present. Use five-year steps.

Bar Graph

| Name | | Date | Problem 20-2 |

Create a line graph showing how the price of the basic automobile has increased since 1940. Use five-year steps.

Line Graph

Name		Date	

Create a pictorial graph showing the enrollment in each grade of your school. Let each symbol represent 25 students.

Picture Graph

| Name | | Date | Problem
20-4 |

3X Ø $\frac{1}{2}$

3X R $\frac{3}{4}$

1

1

2 $\frac{3}{8}$

$\frac{3}{16}$ FILLET WELDS

BRACKET
$\frac{3}{8}$ STEEL PLATE

Draw the orthographic views necessary to describe the assembly and fabrication of the object. Use the correct symbols for the welding information specified. Welds are to be made on both sides of the joint.

Name		Date
	Bracket	

Problem
21-1

SINGLE GUIDE
3/8 STEEL PLATE

4×Ø1/4

3/8

1 5/8

1/2

1 1/8

3/4

13/16

3

3/8

Ø1/2

1 1/2

3/16 FILLET WELDS

1 1/2

2

3/8

3/8

Draw the orthographic views necessary to describe the assembly and fabrication of the object. Use the correct symbols for the welding information specified. Welds are to be made on both sides of the joint.

Single Guide

Name

Date

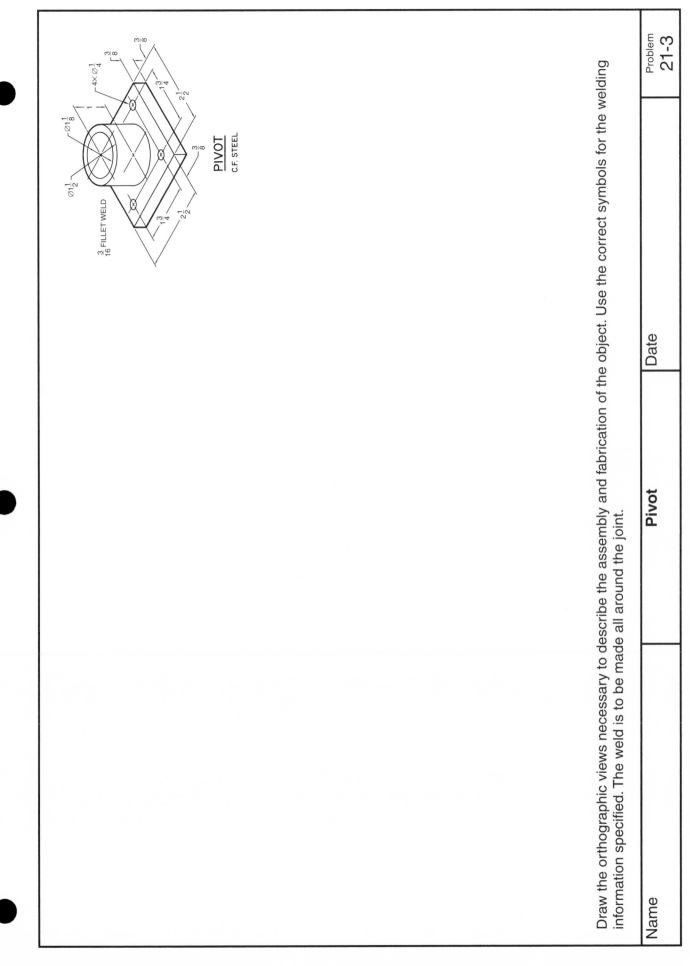

PIVOT
C.F. STEEL

Draw the orthographic views necessary to describe the assembly and fabrication of the object. Use the correct symbols for the welding information specified. The weld is to be made all around the joint.

Name		Pivot	Date	Problem 21-3

OFFSET GUIDE
1/4 STEEL PLATE

3/16 FILLET WELDS

Draw the orthographic views necessary to describe the assembly and fabrication of the object. Use the correct symbols for the welding information specified. Welds are to be made on both sides of each vertical piece.

Name		Offset Guide	Date	Problem 21-4

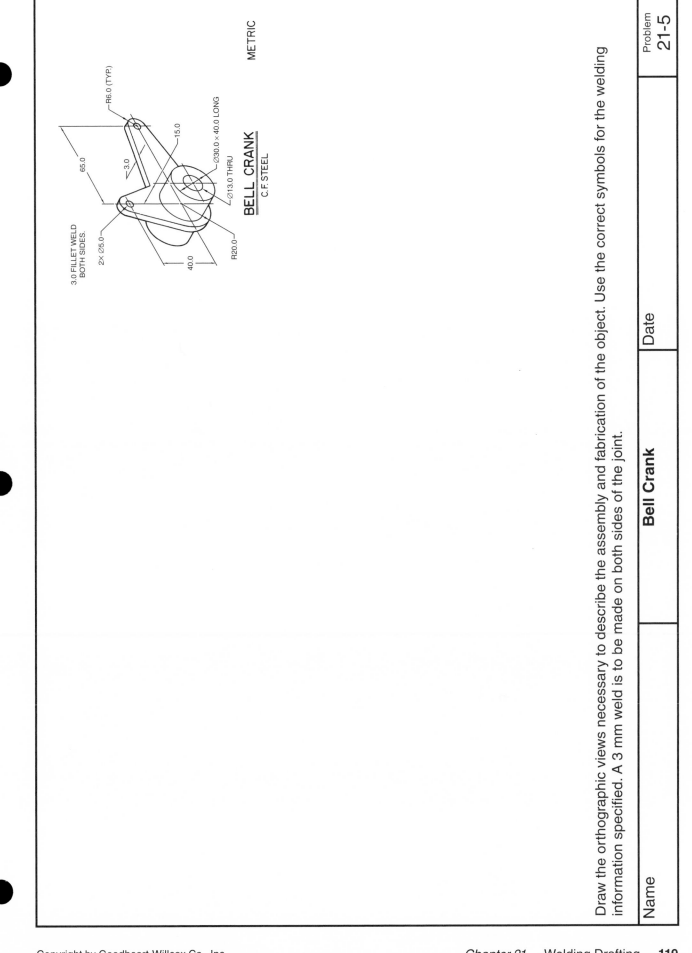

METRIC

R6.0 (TYP.)

65.0

3.0

15.0

3.0 FILLET WELD
BOTH SIDES.

∅30.0 × 40.0 LONG

∅13.0 THRU

BELL CRANK
C.F. STEEL

2× ∅5.0

40.0

R20.0

Draw the orthographic views necessary to describe the assembly and fabrication of the object. Use the correct symbols for the welding information specified. A 3 mm weld is to be made on both sides of the joint.

Name	Date
Bell Crank	Problem **21-5**

Draw a 4" long hexagonal head bolt and nut with 3/4-10UNC-2 threads. Draw a 4" long square head bolt and nut with the same thread specifications. Use simplified thread representations.

| Name | | **Bolts and Nuts** | Date | Problem
22-1 |

Draw a 3" long hexagonal head bolt and nut with 1-8UNC-2 threads. Draw a 3" long square head bolt and nut with the same thread specifications. Use simplified thread representations.

Name		Date	Problem 22-2
	Bolts and Nuts		

Symbols

Plug

Lightbulb

Switch

Make a schematic diagram of a desk lamp.

Name

Date

Desk Lamp Schematic

Prepare a schematic diagram of a two-cell flashlight.

Flashlight Schematic

Name

Date

Draw a wiring diagram of your bedroom.

Wiring Diagram

Problem
23-3

Name

Date

Make a scale drawing of the school drafting room. Use a scale of 1/4" = 1'-0".

Room Layout

Name

Date

Draw a floor plan of your home or apartment.

Floor Plan

Name

Date

Problem
24-2

Design and draw a floor plan for a small vacation cabin.

Name		**Vacation Cabin**	Date

Problem
24-3

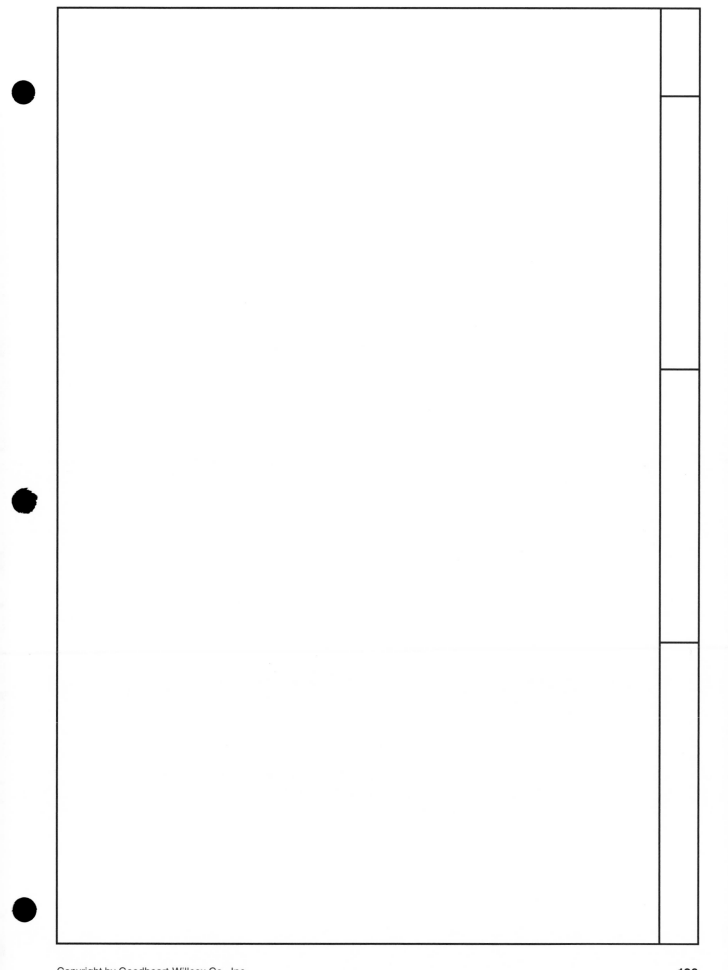